D   MW00462150

Speaking
Across
Generations

Messages That Satisfy Boomers,
Xers, Millennials, Gen Z,
and Beyond

Foreword by Haydn Shaw

An imprint of InterVarsity Press
Downers Grove, Illinois

InterVarsity Press
P.O. Box 1400, Downers Grove, IL 60515-1426
ivpress.com
email@ivpress.com

InterVarsity Press® is the book-publishing division of InterVarsity Christian Fellowship/USA®, a movement
of students and faculty active on campus at hundreds of universities, colleges, and schools of nursing in the
United States of America, and a member movement of the International Fellowship of Evangelical Students.
For information about local and regional activities, visit intervarsity.org.

All Scripture quotations, unless otherwise indicated, are taken from The Holy Bible, New International
Version®, NIV®. Copyright © 1973, 1978, 1984, 2011 by Biblica, Inc.™ Used by permission of Zondervan. All
rights reserved worldwide. www.zondervan.com. The "NIV" and "New International Version" are
trademarks registered in the United States Patent and Trademark Office by Biblica, Inc.™

While any stories in this book are true, some names and identifying information may have been changed to
protect the privacy of individuals.

All data visualizations, unless otherwise noted, designed by Summer Verwers. All research data, unless
otherwise noted, conducted and published by Barna Group and used by permission.

The publisher cannot verify the accuracy or functionality of website URLs used in this book beyond the date
of publication.

Cover design and image composite: David Fassett
Interior design: Daniel van Loon
Images: silhouette of man's head: © CSA Images / Getty Images
        man, woman, large thought bubble: © Klaus Vedfelt / Digital Vision / Getty Images

ISBN 978-1-5140-0308-4 (print)
ISBN 978-1-5140-0309-1 (digital)

Printed in the United States of America ∞

Library of Congress Cataloging-in-Publication Data
A catalog record for this book is available from the Library of Congress.

P 25 24 23 22 21 20 19 18 17 16 15 14 13 12 11 10 9 8 7 6 5 4 3 2 1

Y 40 39 38 37 36 35 34 33 32 31 30 29 28 27 26 25 24 23 22

To my bride, Eboni, and our boys, Dylan, Daniel, and Dixon.

Thank you all for supporting me through

this research and writing.

Contents

Foreword by Haydn Shaw — *vii*

Introduction — *1*

1: Generational Science and Its Many Benefits — *5*

2: Becoming a Generational Polyglot — *20*

3: Language Is More — *31*

4: Good News for Elders — *42*

5: Good News for Baby Boomers — *53*

6: Good News for Generation X — *65*

7: Good News for Millennials — *79*

8: Good News for Generation Z — *98*

9: The Family of God — *113*

10: Intergenerational in Everything We Do — *121*

Conclusion — *135*

Acknowledgments — *140*

Appendix A: About the Research — *142*

Appendix B: How to Apply this Research — *144*

Appendix C: The Intergenerational God — *146*

Appendix D: An Intergenerational People — *153*

Appendix E: An Intergenerational Gospel — *157*

Notes — *164*

Foreword

Haydn Shaw, author of Generational IQ

Preaching changes, but sometimes preachers do not. Younger preachers must learn how to communicate to older generations, but sometimes we quit learning to communicate to the generations now younger than us. Sometimes we do not adapt quickly enough because we miss the earliest signs that the younger generation is beginning to tune us out. Usually, it is because we are comfortable with the approach we use, even if we learned it twenty-five years ago. Whatever the reason, preaching to five generations is complicated, and the message is too important to get tangled in the packaging.

Speaking Across Generations shows you how to learn different generational languages so you can have a vibrant preaching ministry across multiple generations. Here are four reasons you need this book:

1. ***You need this original research on how to preach to each of the five generations.*** I get asked how to adjust preaching to each generation. Darrell provides the best answer. Darrell and I talked about how generational research can enhance

preaching, what is working in churches, and where to find the best barbeque in Atlanta. Darrell and the Barna team's new research will shake up your thinking with solid data. This is some of the most helpful sociological research on preaching yet.

2. **Speaking Across Generations *will save you countless arguments.*** It's a blessing from God that we live thirty years longer, but never have we had five generations of adults in church. Navigating five generations means that no matter how you preach, multiple generations will criticize your sermons. This book will save countless arguments because you can thank them for their interest and feedback and then point the critics to this data.

3. ***You need Darrell's millennial perspective on preaching and the church.*** Most preaching books come from older generations. We need younger voices to join the conversation. Apple taught us that younger generations respond to design even more readily than older ones do. We need younger generations to show us sermon design hacks so our packaging does not block people from hearing the message.

4. ***You need the planning tool.*** Life stage is the cutting edge of generational research. Today you can't do generations well without it. Darrell shows you how to utilize it to plan messages. He provides a tool that is worth the price of the book. Use it each week to build your sermon applications, and it will ratchet up your sermons to another level.

How do you adjust your preaching to each generation? Look no further for the answer. *Speaking Across Generations* has provided the answer key and just possibly the key to your staying fresh and vibrant in ministry over the long haul.

Introduction

It was just a Wednesday, but the struggles of that day would be more valuable to the future of my preaching ministry than I could understand at the time. I was a twenty-something youth pastor at a megachurch. I was also an associate minister who often had to fill in for the senior pastor. On one Wednesday I experienced the vast complexity of my role. Early that morning, I was responsible for teaching during the chapel service of the elementary academy our church supported. Then, at noon, I was asked to fill in for midday Bible study, which is mainly attended by people in our congregation older than sixty years of age. That evening, I taught the teenagers during our church's weekly Bible study.

I was exhausted by day's end. I had taught almost 150 people the Bible in one day. Their ages ranged from kindergarten through high school to senior adulthood. The challenge of the day though was that I taught the exact same Bible lesson in all three experiences. With only enough time to prepare one message, I taught that same message to multiple generations. Even without distinct notes for each, the teaching seemed to be well received and easily understood. I did not notice it then, but I was learning on the job how to communicate effectively to multiple generations.

That Wednesday was perhaps only eclipsed by an even more overwhelming Sunday. I was still a twenty-something youth pastor and associate minister at the same church. It was during the second of three Sunday morning services we host at our main campus. I was in the middle of a sermon in teen service when an emergency happened. Our senior pastor had gotten stuck in his travel between our multisite church campuses. It was time for the sermon in the adult worship service. He was not going to make it back in time. I had to preach in his place. A leader politely interrupted teen church to inform us of the emergency. She insisted that I complete my message in five minutes because I had to be in the main sanctuary to preach in ten minutes.

So, with a huge lump in my throat and my heart beating through my chest, I did just that. I was whisked from a chapel of 100 middle and high school students to a sanctuary of 2,000 adults of all ages. Thanks be to God, I lived to preach another day. I did not notice it then, but I was learning to communicate effectively to multiple generations by baptism through fire.

If you get anxiety just reading these words, then you understand the anxiety I felt preaching through those experiences. I began preaching at seventeen years old. Reared in a strong, large, Black church situated in Atlanta, Georgia, I have traveled a unique path through ministry. For more than a decade I have been in full-time vocational ministry for the church I grew up in. After serving for five years as youth pastor, I became campus pastor of one campus within a multisite context. It has been a burdensome delight to grow from a teen preacher through my twenties and now into my thirties, making every effort I can to connect with audiences of all ages.

I am not certain, but I am hopeful that as you read you will see that these pages, this research, and these concepts were laid out for you. The goal of this book is to explore one demographic factor that even audience members may be unaware of—the generational factor. This book shares the characteristics, skills, and rhetorical strategies of effective intergenerational preaching. We will explore how generational science can inform how a preacher crafts sermons to reach people of different age groups. The spirit of this book is intended to improve the ability of readers to communicate more effectively with people of different generations. I will share my struggles and experiences, we will examine some research, and together we will move forward more encouraged to do the work it will take to leave no generation unreached by our message.

Generational Science
and Its Many Benefits

It nearly shook me to my core when I finally noticed what was happening. By this time, I had been promoted. No longer was I a twenty-something youth pastor giving oversight to students at four campuses. Now, I was an almost thirty-something campus pastor responsible for shepherding one campus. The church campus I was pastoring was diverse in the ages of the people who were actively attending. I would regularly ask myself, "How did this happen?"

I feared losing the respect of people old enough to be my parents and grandparents. I pondered so many anxious questions like: Would they take me seriously? Could my normally silly personality be viewed as juvenile? Could they accept Holy Communion from someone wearing Jordan 1s and slim-fit jeans? *Maybe I should wear a robe and be more serious*, I thought. *But then*, I feared, *I might lose myself and my organic connection with those in my own age group.* Not to mention that my years as a youth pastor lingered in my mind as the glory days where I could easily connect with an age group otherwise foreign to many adult communicators—teenagers. I was not ready to let go of whatever it was about me that helped teens see me as someone they enjoyed hearing.

For almost seven years, I pastored and preached with these thoughts influencing almost everything I did. One Sunday, I would wear a cassock and wingtip boots. The next Sunday, I would wear a T-shirt and jeans. My frantic wardrobe choices reflected on the outside the tug of war I was feeling on the inside. After years of fretting, the generations kept coming and the Lord kept blessing our fellowship. Finally, the Spirit led me to investigate and inform myself on what it meant to preach effectively to all generations.

Pastors and preachers of all ages have experienced anxieties like mine. Some well-known faces have undergone wardrobe changes. Others have massively renovated their pulpits and platforms. Preaching novices have undertaken years of academic rigor. Then there are those who have apprenticed and served faithfully on church staffs to gain much-needed experience. The seasoned preacher still wants to appeal to the young. The preaching phenom yearns for the respect of the aged. All the above, and more, are practical moves preachers of varying capacities make to maintain their ability to connect with their audience.

Perhaps you picked up this book hoping to learn something that would help you reach a generation or age group you fear you are missing in your church. If so, I ask you to sit with the findings and concepts in these pages before you do anything else. Prayerfully engage the content before you makeover your look, upgrade your stage, or hire more people from the generation you hope to reach. If you can help it. For as long as it takes you to read this book, put your fears and anxieties on pause. I am only asking you to consider doing what I have done too.

The findings in this book stem from insights I have gained from focus groups within the metro-Atlanta congregation[1] where I serve and results from a survey conducted across America. The nationwide survey was uniquely developed and organized by me in collaboration with the research team at Barna Group, who disseminated it nationwide. In addition to the questions we asked, we played audio snippets from sermons of multiple preachers. We then correlated the clips preferred with the age and generation of the person who selected them. What we discovered is that generations have their own language they prefer to hear from communicators. I will name these languages and give examples of how to implement them in the wording and reasoning of our sermons.

Before we get there though, let's look at what I learned from my congregation. As I put my own anxieties aside, I learned that the characteristics that made me an effective intergenerational preacher were not primarily aesthetic at all. My worries about wardrobe were not as important as I feared. The stage could have used some upgrades, but people continued to attend and happily look at a traditional pulpit with a wooden podium. What I learned is that there were traits that the people in my church most appreciated. These traits were valued highly by people across every generation. I learned from my congregation what I was doing by mistake and without intentionality. Gaining clarity on these traits helped me to focus my efforts on effectiveness and not aesthetics.

Characteristics of Effective Intergenerational Preaching

I conducted focus groups of three to eight people per generation and surveyed the entire congregation. I met with elders, boomers, Gen Xers, millennials, and Gen Zers. After conducting the focus groups, the characteristics of an effective intergenerational preacher became clear: one who is characterized by Bible-based content, aha moments, no emotionalism or manipulation, simplicity, and teaching. To be fair, these insights came from people who were predominantly African American, professing Christians, and members of our church. The main demographical factor though is that they were generationally diverse. Before we explore what each generation uniquely desires, we will look at what all generations desire in their preacher.

People come to church to hear a specific perspective on life: *people want to hear the Bible and its contents in preaching*. It could be that Bible-based content was the most prominent mark because all the people identify as Christians. Or because it is a stated and apparent value of our church. Nevertheless, it is encouraging to know that listeners wanted to hear the Bible. This does not guarantee that the listeners believe in the validity of Scripture or that they will agree with theological principles. That people want to hear the Bible preached does not mean they believe the Bible is inerrant. However, it does indicate that churchgoers value the contents of Scripture when they listen to preaching. People log onto or walk into a church for the purpose of hearing something distinct from what they have heard from other platforms or mediums of communication.

The next characteristic of effective intergenerational preaching is for a person *to experience an aha moment*. People indicated that these moments can be had by way of clarity of understanding or a conviction to change their lives. People desire a clear understanding of how to apply the Word to everyday life. Megan the millennial said she desired "a sermon that is clear . . . that I can understand." Alex the Gen Xer said he wanted the preacher to "teach and educate me on the Word and to explain" it to him. Brenda the boomer simply stated that she wanted "understanding." Xander the Gen Zer said, "Preaching that I understand without having to think so much that I'm missing the sermon trying to understand."

I chose to describe these as aha moments, which are those times when the hearer gets it. People do not want to come to church and feel confused about what is being done or said. Even if they experience one aha moment per sermon they hear, it is worth the time given to the sermon. People remember moments more than they recall words, outlines, or arguments. As preachers we should spend our minutes crafting sermons that create moments.

The third characteristic of effective intergenerational preaching is that it should be *done without emotionalism and/or manipulation.* People can detect emotionalism and sniff out manipulation. Many hearers are suspicious of a preacher's lack of preparedness as the reason for emotionalism. They fear getting money is the aim of manipulation. All generations despise selfish motives in preaching. Emotionalism and manipulation turn off the hearer and prevent, or uproot, an effective transference of the gospel or biblical message. Our sermons can be emotive without veering into emotionalism. We can aim at preaching to move people without trying to manipulate them. There is a distinct difference.

The fourth and fifth characteristics of effective intergenerational preaching are *simplicity* and *teaching.* All generations desire simple teaching. This does not mean that the congregants want the preacher to be a simpleton or for their message to lack depth. Depth does not mean mystifying. Their desire for simplicity lies more in their ability to grasp the message than in the preacher's depth. The deeper the concept, the more clearly people need for the preacher to explain it. For all groups, a preacher's ability to break down complex biblical content so simply that a child could understand is important. If a child can understand it, that increases the probability that an adult can understand too. However, just because an adult can understand it, there is no guarantee that a child can. In John 21, Jesus told Peter to "feed my lambs" before he told him to "take care of my sheep." Lambs are little sheep. Younger sheep. Simplicity of understanding means all listeners can learn from the message. Our people want to be taught; so, as preachers, let us teach. These desires for simplicity and teaching align with the one competency offered by Paul in the qualifications of a bishop (1 Tim 3:2; Titus 1:9).

The beauty of preaching is like many of life's noble pursuits—no matter how good we may get at it we can always get better. Mastery is elusive, but we can be committed practitioners. I am committed to a better practice of the five traits we just covered. Working on these things are more important, it turns out, than whether I wear wingtips or Jordan 1s.

You Can Do This

Are you reading this book because you want to nourish the minds, hearts, and souls of the people you influence? I believe so. Some of you have been serving hearty sermonic content and want to keep doing so. You have done well. Your voices are respected. You have received five-star reviews on your preaching for years. You value the sweat equity invested into your work so much that you want to keep growing. You are a tinkerer. Others look at you and say, "Wow, look at how well you communicate." However, you hear yourself and think, *This is good, but it can get better.* You also sense the palates of your potential listeners are more complex as the days go by. While you have some nonnegotiables that can never change, you are willing to change some things about your approach to remain effective. This is the continuing pursuit of anyone who is effective in anything, including preaching.

For others, you know that the reviews of your preaching have not been so flattering. You recall a time when it seemed you were effective, but you blinked, and times have changed. You have not accepted ineffectiveness as your fate. You have tried to tinker, but it seems like you keep fixing the wrong cog in the process. Despite what you do, there is a growing fear of disconnect. You are not reaching your audience like you wished that you could. You try to reason it away, but your gut feels the pain. *Maybe I am getting too old for this*, you think. Or, *I am so young and in over my head*. This fear of losing your cutting edge could make you envy others who seem to be magnetic. *What are they doing that I am not? What are they doing that I cannot?* Becoming distracted by another preacher's artistry can sidetrack you from the science you can study and apply.

The Science and Art of It

The connection between science and art impacts every profession. There is a science to filmmaking, but Ryan Coogler has unique artistic ability. Hit TV shows have scientific ingredients, but Shonda Rhimes has the secret sauce. There is a science to leadership, ergo John Maxwell. There is also an art to leadership, ergo John Maxwell. There is a science to marketing. Then there is Coca-Cola, a marketing firm masquerading as a beverage company. All gymnasts are taught the science of tumbling, but somewhere along the way, Simone Biles separated from the pack. Political science can be studied, but there is something about the charisma of John F. Kennedy or Barack Obama. There are fundamentals to shooting a basketball, then there is Steph Curry's flick of the wrist, quick release, and endless range. Artists should be appreciated for their uniqueness. However, world-class talents should not overshadow scientific laws, proven techniques, and learnable principles. These can be applied by all, including you and me. So let us work on our skills to increase the effectiveness of our preaching.

Effective preaching only happens strategically. Even the communicators who make it look easy have put in hard work. Extemporaneous speaking seems to happen off the top of the head but note that the speaker's head is not an empty one. It is filled with experiential knowledge, proven facts, and tricks of the trade. Preachers who speak without immediate preparation can only do so because of compounded preparation. They did not need to get ready in that moment. The best preachers are always getting ready long before "the moment." *Communicators*

You may never be able to emulate the vocal imprint of your favorite preacher. You may never be able to reproduce their charisma. I have tried to do both and failed. That should not be your goal anyway. Yours is a unique vocal imprint. You have a unique personality. Your desire to be effective should account for these truths.

Knowing Your Audience

As a preacher prepares their messages, knowing their audience is key. When you know your audience, you can better understand the lens they view the world through. Knowing their worldview is vital to reaching them. While they want to hear what you are saying, their hearts and minds lie behind the walls of their worldviews. To reach them, you must scale, knock down, crawl under, or circumvent their walls, many of which the audience does not even know they have thrown up.

Your approach as a preacher is reflected in the intentional rhetoric and reasoning you use in a message. This rhetoric and reasoning are based on the demographics of your audience. As a communicator, aim to tailor your approach to uniquely overcome the defensive mechanisms of the audience's worldview. Studying the demographics of an audience requires a layered approach. If a person is complex, an audience of people is even more complex. Most demographic criteria can be learned. Gender, racial, educational, and socioeconomic factors can be easily discovered. A brief conversation with the right questions can also reveal political, religious, and ethnic cultural factors. These demographic factors are all important in studying your audience. But the goal of this book is to explore the demographic factor that even audience members may be unaware of—the generational factor.

Take a moment to write down what you think are the percentages of each age group in your flock. Do not worry about being technical with the age brackets and generational nicknames. We will cover that next.

Generations See the Same Things Differently

The generational lens is vital to the way people receive communication. Wise communicators take the time to understand the generations. Generational science is important for effective communication. For example, say I have been asked to speak at a youth basketball league's award ceremony. My idea is to take principles from the greatest basketball player ever and use them to inspire the youth. *This should not be hard to do*, I think to myself. That is, until I arrive. Then I realize that the players are accompanied by their families. I then notice that many of their family members are older than them. Why is this key? Because I built my speech around LeBron James. The millennials might disagree in favor of Kobe Bryant. The Gen Xers might disagree in favor of Michael Jordan. The baby boomers would prefer Larry Bird or Magic Johnson. The elders would argue that Wilt Chamberlain is the greatest. It would not be wise of me to trudge forward ignoring generational science.

Generational perspectives influence the lens through which basketball fans determine greatness. It would be wise for me to think creatively. I could adjust easily. I might decide to use my introduction to create humor around the tension. I could start by polling the room. I could even say, "The principles that make basketball players great keep showing up, generation after generation." In that way generational science can help me turn a speech into an engaging intergenerational experience.

Generations are shaped by the social events taking place during their coming-of-age years. Agreeing on the greatest basketball player ever is not a serious issue. However, there are more serious issues that generations see differently. Political perspectives, gender roles in society, the nature of marriage, and how to use money are all serious issues. Questions about what activities are age appropriate. Disagreements about the use of corporal punishment. Notions of wrong and right. Civil rights debates and initiatives. All of these can be viewed through generational science because during each generation's coming-of-age years, these issues and more were being played out in society in ways unique to every other generation's experience. Do not fret—generational science can be learned. You can grow in your generational intelligence. It is simply the study of different cohorts of people born within a certain time frame and what shaped their age group in their worldviews.

The Generations

First, let's look at how each living generation is named and defined. There is some variation in the exact years where sociologists and pop culture draw these lines, but here is how the Barna Group defines the generations.[2] The *elders* were born in 1945 and before. *Baby boomers* were born between 1946 and 1964. *Generation X* was born between 1965 and 1983. *Millennials* were born between 1984 and 1998. *Generation Z*—which may eventually be renamed, just as Gen Y became millennials—was born between 1999 to 2015. The generation born since 2016 is tentatively named *alpha.*

Second, it is important that we know some facts about how the generations stack up against each other. For example, Generation X is the smallest generation in American history. Millennials, on the other hand, are now the largest generation in American history, a title previously held by the baby boomers. As boomers aged and began to pass on, millennials were coming of age. So not only do millennial births outnumber boomer births, but the population numbers in 2021 reflect this too. Baby boomers are the only generation to be officially named by the Census Bureau.[3] Other generations pick up their names from pop culture and sociologists along the way.

Finally, gaining an understanding of the spiritual and religious dynamics and forces that shaped the collective experience of each age cohort is essential to preaching effectively. In her book *When Anything Goes*, Leslie Williams says, "In the late 1980s . . . the world was now 'post-Christian.' Sophisticated and intelligent people no longer believed in the Judeo-Christian metanarrative or the Resurrection."[4] This is important context to understanding how the generations relate to each other. While elders maintained a predominantly Christian society and may have raised their boomer children with these values, much of the religious experience shifted in the '60s and '70s. It could be said that boomers started the American post-Christian age, Gen Xers championed it, millennials were raised in post-Christianity, and Gen Z are children of post-Christianity. Barna sometimes refers to Generation Z as the "blank slate" generation—the first in which a substantial proportion were raised without any connection to religious or spiritual practices or belief. This blank slate can be a positive if we choose to see it that way.

Generations as People Groups

Each generation should be understood as a distinct people group. How you respond to this claim will determine how you receive the rest of the ideas in this book. Each generation has its own language, culture, and life stage needs. The language and culture of a generation are static; they go with them through life. The life stage needs of a generation are dynamic; they grow with them through life. According to Ken Baker in his book *Beyond People Groups*, "The Lausanne committee uses this definition of 'people group': a people group is the largest group within which the gospel can spread as a church-planting movement without encountering barriers of understanding or acceptance."[5] The most common application of this is with ethnic people groups. It is true that a church can be planted in a Haitian community and spread without language or cultural barriers. Even though Haitians are not monolithic, Haitian culture has generalities that its people understand. A church can also be planted among millennials and spread without language or culture barriers. Generations, like ethnicities, are not monolithic within themselves, but they do share commonalities of experience and perspective. This is key because as we progress further into the twenty-first century, ethnicities may start to blend while generations become more distinct.

The word *gospel* means "good news." The gospel of Jesus is good news whenever it is preached, wherever it is preached, and to whomever it is preached. This is a distinct quality of the gospel. Think about it—some good news is good news for a limited time only: a store having a sale, a new blockbuster movie on opening weekend, or the features of the newest model of a vehicle. That good news eventually expires, is surpassed by newer good news, or reaches its manufactured date of obsolescence. Then there is good news restricted to a certain region or jurisdiction, like winters in southern California, low crime rates in affluent zip codes, or spending New Year's Eve in Times Square. California's winters are not good news for New Englanders. People in low-income zip codes do not benefit from the low crime rates in zip codes they cannot afford. Then there is good news that is only good for a select few, like tax laws depending on which political party is in office. With every change in federal taxation some Americans groan while others grin. When the pendulum swings in the other direction, groaners become grinners and grinners start groaning.

The gospel of Jesus is good news for all time, in all places, for all people. There is no era in history, geopolitical territory, or people group where the gospel of Jesus has not been good news. In the Middle Ages, it was good news. In developing countries, it is good news. To every ethnicity, unique subculture, family, or generation, the gospel is good news. However, it must be presented differently depending on the time, place, and group to whom it is preached. This is the essence of contextualization. That is true of generational people groups too.

Viewing generations as people groups might explain why brands generally reach one more effectively than the others. Sears reached the boomers. Walmart and Target reach Gen X. Amazon speaks to millennials. The global pandemic made Amazon's customer base even more intergenerational. Prior to the pandemic though, a higher percentage of millennials had more Amazon Prime accounts than any other generation. Certain brands and businesses better connect with certain generations. This is true of preachers and churches too. Church rosters and seats may be filled with

people predominantly from one generation. In some church traditions, there are even nicknames for congregations that have a generational majority. For example, a gray-headed church is one made
up mostly of the aging and elderly. Why do some businesses and
churches reach one generation more effectively than the others?
I believe it is because people hear in their native generational
tongue and receive all communication through a native generational lens. This is not just a hunch.

C. S. Lewis writes, "If you were sent to the Bantus you would be
taught their language and traditions. You need similar teaching
about the language and mental habits of your own . . . fellow
countrymen."[6] Lewis claims a preacher needs to understand their
own people. To become more effective, we could learn more about
the language and mentality of people in our own ethnic people
group. Remember, generations are people groups too. As preachers
we could also learn more about the language and perspectives of
our own and another generational group.

Intergenerational Versus Multigenerational

To be intergenerational differs from being multigenerational. *Inter-*
means "together." *Multi-* means "several." We could have several
generations present without them being together. A multi-locked
door means there are several individual locks on a door. An
interlocking chain means links come together to form a stronger
bond. The world was not created to be multigenerational. The
world was created to be intergenerational. Brands are feverishly
working to become intergenerational. Major world cities are
building themselves into intergenerational hubs. The church, too,
was founded to be intergenerational.

In *Generational IQ*, Haydn Shaw asserts, "To fulfill God's pur-
poses in our generations, we will need to figure out how to speak

the languages of the different generations. The real God is amazing, so we need to be able to explain Him to the next generation."[7] Viewing generations as people groups will make our communication more strategic. We can learn to speak to the missing generations in our churches. As preachers we can grow to explain God, preach the gospel, and teach the Bible in the native tongue of each generation. We can learn to communicate to each group alone. We could even develop the ability to communicate to all generations when they are present together. That is the essence of effective intergenerational communication.

Becoming
a Generational Polyglot

Growing in our generational intelligence will develop us into generational polyglots. A polyglot is a person who knows and can use several languages. We can grow from being generationally unilingual (speaking one language fluently) to generationally bilingual (speaking two languages fluently) and then to generationally polylingual (speaking multiple languages fluently).

All of us are already generationally unilingual. We speak our own generation's language fluently. Becoming generationally bilingual may mean also speaking the language of the generation before us. This could be a result of having been raised by parents, educated by teachers, or mentored by leaders from the previous generation. Becoming generationally polylingual will require more of us. Why? Because we would have to intentionally learn the way another generation speaks, one beyond our own and the one that raised us. It takes work to understand the language of the generation that came after you. It takes even more work to understand a generation that does not fall directly before or after yours. For example, a boomer might easily speak the language of boomers and elders, while struggling to speak the language of Gen Zers. Or a millennial might better understand Gen Xers than they do boomers and elders.

Culture and Preaching

Building a new home is as fun as it is stressful. In 2014, my young family grew from four to five with the arrival of a new baby boy. Our apartment was no longer enough for a family with three rambunctious boys. We needed a house. God provided one too. When we found our house, it was already being built. We got to pick some last-minute details about the design to help make it our own. But making the house our home far exceeded the color of carpet that we chose. It was not until we moved in and settled down that we could begin to really envision what we wanted our home to be. The décor, paint, room designs, dining table, and furniture all contribute to the uniqueness of our home. The more important things though are immaterial. Love, unity, forgiveness, dialogues, and mealtimes are what shape the culture of a home. The builder gave us a house; our choices made it a home.

The opening chapters of Genesis are clear that God created the heavens and the earth. On the sixth day, God created humans. God made the world, but as Andy Crouch says in his book *Culture Making*, "Culture is what human beings make of the world."[1] Culture is the life we make in community with the lives around us. Culture is the reciprocal expression of individual identity with communal ideals. Individuals affect the community as the community impacts individuals. Culture is the result of the rhythm of life of a person in syncopation with the lives of a people. So, what does that say about the inherent goodness or badness of culture? Is culture good? Yes, at its best. Is culture bad? Yes, at its worst. Culture in a vacuum is amoral, neither good nor bad.

In *Christ and Culture*, H. Richard Niebuhr outlines a taxonomy of five relationships between the two subjects of his title: Christ against culture, Christ of culture, Christ above culture, Christ and culture in paradox, and Christ transforming culture. Douglas Webster adds another nuance to the relationship between the two in his book *Outposts of Hope*. He ascribes to a Christ for culture strategy. A Christ for culture perspective recalls God's pre-fall approval of creation when he "saw that it was good" (Gen 1:10, 12, 18, 21, 25; see also Gen 1:31). The intrinsic goodness of creation was reinforced by God's approval of it. A Christ for culture perspective views culture as an extension of God's created order. Even after creation was tainted by sin, God's love sparked the promise of the complete redemption of creation through Christ (Rom 8:18-22). If culture is composed of food, language, music, customs, fashion, family constructs, gender roles, and so on, then it and all its parts are redeemable in Christ.

Every redeemed part of creation will be on the New Earth. There will be trees on the New Earth. Those trees will be beautiful, healthy, and lush. There will also be culture. There will be rich, vibrant, and textured culture on the New Earth. Culture then is as much an amoral part of God's good creation as the trees. Since the blood of Jesus gives promise to the redemption of creation, culture will be redeemed with the trees.

The Forgotten Sphere of Culture

A redemptive Christ for culture characteristic in preaching will benefit the believer and non-believer alike. Redemptive preaching will guard against separating the believer from the culture because the believer is called out of the world system, not out of culture (Jn 17:15-18; 2 Cor 6:17). It will also guard against alienating the non-believer from the church. Though the non-believer must turn away from sin, not everything in culture is sinful.

Like Christ, believers have not been called to withdraw from culture but to engage in it. Jesus himself prayed, "I do not pray that You should take them out of the world" (Jn 17:15 NKJV). A solid theology of preaching does not make the pious choice between two polar extremes: totally engrossed in culture or completely withdrawn from it. "Peter's Christ for culture strategy includes what Christ opposes in our sinful, broken, and fallen human culture, not for the sake of opposition, but for the sake of redemption and reconciliation,"[2] says Webster. A Christ for culture perspective will require us to view culture and all its spheres as intrinsically good and completely redeemable.

In his book *Preaching with Cultural Intelligence*, Matthew Kim introduces different cultural spheres. Kim persuades the reader to use cultural intelligence in preaching by considering the spheres of culture. He mentions denominations, ethnicities, genders, locations, and religions as spheres of culture. Kim acknowledges the ubiquitous nature of culture and that "defining culture succinctly and cogently is quite tricky."[3] However, he explains that culture is at its core "a way of thinking" that influences "a way of behaving" that becomes "a way of living."[4]

The culture of a generation is the forgotten sphere of culture. Generational cultures are as viable as the other spheres. Culture is composed of food, language, music, customs, fashion, family constructs, and gender roles. Thus, every generation has a distinct culture. The generation a person was born in influences how he or she thinks, behaves, and lives. Effective intergenerational preaching requires generational cultural intelligence.

The generational sphere of culture can be seen within an ethnically homogenous group. Black people are not monolithic. Some are politically conservative while others are politically liberal. Asian people are not monolithic. Hong Kong is a totally different world than the Philippines. Ethnic people groups are tremendously diverse in other areas. Hispanic people could be introverts or extroverts. The French are composed of intellectuals and artists. A room full of Russian people would land in different quadrants all over the DISC personality profile. The spheres of location and gender can create cultural nuances within ethnicities or nationalities, meaning you can get a room full of European people and subdivide them based on their gender and native country. The same is true generationally. In a room full of Americans, one could subdivide them generationally. Those generational groups will likely have distinct cultures from the others.

Interestingly, the generational sphere of culture could also be seen in an ethnically heterogeneous group. In an interracial group you can subdivide it generationally. How? Generational spheres can converge even where ethnic spheres may diverge. Due to globalization, media, and technology, an Asian American millennial likely has more in common with an African American millennial than either of them has in common with their boomer parents or grandparents. It is likely that I have more in common culturally with a smartphone-carrying millennial in Australia than I do with the grandmother who powdered and pampered my butt.

Preaching with Generational Intelligence

One of my mentors, Thomas, had a disagreement with his adult son, Jameson. Thomas is a career public servant, executive-level leader, PhD family man, and baby boomer. Jameson is a millennial, one of three children, a single father of two, and climbing through the police department ranks. Jameson leans on his parents to help with his children. Thomas and his wife, Claire, are glad to support Jameson and give extra care to their grandchildren. A conflict arose when Thomas approached his son to hold him accountable. Thomas noticed Jameson faltering in some ways where he felt he should exercise more wisdom. Jameson's response to his dad's advice was, "Can we not be father and son right now? Can you just approach me man to man?" Thomas, startled by the request, replied "No, I cannot. You have to understand authority and my role in your life as your father." Where Jameson desired dialogue among mutual parties, Thomas desired to establish a clear line of distinction that colored what was said and how it should be received.

Who was wrong? Neither. Who was right? Neither. Who was being true to how they viewed that conversation based on their generation's values? Both. Who could have increased the success of the interchange by trying to see things through the other's eyes? Both. Thomas was convinced that a hierarchy of honor must be considered when it comes to family matters, so he chose to use authority instead of collaboration. Jameson saw collaboration and dialogue as the only real means to a solution. Both were right from their generational vantage point. The true test of these different perspectives will be when Jameson's son grows up and requests the same of him. Will he respond like a father? Or will he respond like a millennial who is a father? There is a difference.

The defining events of each American generation molded that generation's culture by shaping its values, perspective, and language. Generations are distinct because they came of age with political, cultural, and spiritual factors unique to their experience. The zeitgeist of a generation molds its culture as it seeks independence from the preceding generation and before it accepts responsibility for the succeeding generation. Chances are many of our cultural tastes were molded during a specific window of time in our lives. And even when our palates evolve, a blast from the past can always give us a cozy sense of nostalgia. Perhaps our political views have been shaped by the first few times we were old enough to vote. What about media narratives and the stories of history makers from our formative years? How much have they shaped the context of the way we frame and tell the story of our lives? Despite how old boomers get, nostalgia will always take them back to the '50s, '60s, and '70s; Gen Xers think back to the '70s, '80s, and '90s; and millennials to the '80s, '90s, and aughts.

People subconsciously take their generation's values, perspectives, and language with them through every stage of life. This generational lens affects how all forms of communication are interpreted too. One need only look at marketing strategies during a generation's peak earning years and buying potential to see how they perceive messaging. Marketers target each generation by communicating in their language. Preaching is a specialized form of communication and is evaluated as much through the lens of the person's generational culture as their ethnic culture. Marketers know this implicitly. Preachers must learn it and practice it wisely.

The values and perspectives of a generation are important for the delivery and receptivity of preaching. In *Preaching with Variety* Jeffrey Arthurs says, "Skillful rhetoricians analyze the audience to determine their existing beliefs and values, and then they use those presuppositions in their own persuasion."[5] Effective communication cannot happen by mistake. Communicators must have a strategy of persuasion that includes approach, tone, and word choice. This strategy can be crafted best when the lenses of the listeners have been tried on by the communicator. Knowing what a person values impacts the effectiveness of sermon development and delivery. Remembering that a person's values are influenced through many lenses, including their generational lens, is invaluable. The values and perspectives of a generation formulate the rubric by which a generation unconsciously determines the effectiveness of preaching.

As times change so does the standard of what makes preaching good.[6] If the boomer whose preaching is widely accepted as effective by his generation remains static, he may be deemed ineffective by millennials. How is it that boomers can flock to a preacher that millennials cannot listen to for very long? Is the problem with the preacher? Is it the content? Or are the attention spans of twenty-somethings and thirty-somethings to blame? Many an answer given in response to these questions is steeped in cultural assumptions. Generational intelligence can bring much-needed resolutions to such a range of complex questions.

Most preachers are aware of the importance of cultural sensitivity. We know it would be ineffective for an American-born English-speaking preacher to take the gospel to Southeast Asia with incorrect or unknown cultural assumptions. It is equally as ineffective for a millennial to presume to preach to elders with incorrect or unknown cultural assumptions. In *Preaching to a Post-Everything World*, Zack Eswine states that preaching with cultural assumptions is dangerous because when you "add to these philosophical, economic, political, technological, and religious thoughts of the day . . . what a generation expects relevant preaching to look like both multiplies and diverges."[7] To preach with cultural assumptions is to preach without generational intelligence.

Preaching with generational intelligence must include understanding how the values and perspectives of the generations shape the languages of the generations. Understanding the language of the generation is important because preaching is supposed to communicate yesterday's truths in today's words. The gospel and Scripture are timeless. The language of the age must be timely. Generational intelligence requires an understanding of language. Why? Because one generation's favorite idiom is another's tired cliché.[8] People of one generation insist "a family that prays together, stays together." When people of another generation hear that, they roll their eyes recalling their religious parents who went through a nasty divorce. Preachers who preach without understanding a generation's language "find themselves speaking in a language that is no longer fresh, about concerns that no longer matter to a generation that no longer exists."[9] Even if the generation still exists, it may not be the most prominent or only generation represented in any given audience.

Knowledge of a culture's language improves the preacher's ability to connect with that culture. Robert Smith says, "We must take time to learn and understand *idiomatic expressions* popular in different cultures . . . we have to appreciate the idiomatic expressions, cell-phone language, and the nuances of the communities in which we preach."[10] This is vital because there are no bilingual generational translators, like those who benefit an English-speaking preacher in a Swahili-speaking culture. The preacher herself must be generationally polylingual. She must become a generational polyglot. One can begin to grasp the language of a generation by listening to its songs, watching its movies, reading its books, and studying its history. However, while those are practical ways to help the preacher, such an approach mostly gives the preacher phraseology—and language is more than mere phraseology.

Preaching with generational intelligence requires an intentionality in the preacher to speak from the text in the words, pictures, and ideas of the people being addressed, so that they can hear the text for themselves. The language of a generation goes beyond phraseology to include formulations of thought, which influence the reasoning a group uses. The reasoning a group uses is expressed through rhetoric. This line of thinking gets us closer to heart of what I mean by generational languages.

Preaching with generational intelligence means the preacher knows not only how to delight millennials with colloquialisms but also how to disarm them with persuasion. Why is this important? Because throwing in the newest catch phrase will come across as disingenuous, and millennials can sniff out inauthenticity in a flash. You are more likely to get laughed at—or "cancelled"—than to open their hearts to listen. Tucker explains why the millennial generation, for example, would best hear preaching delivered dialogically: "The emergence of social media in the last ten years has also spawned a preference for dialogue over monologue, discussion over proclamation."[11] Social media users no longer revere the voice of the six o'clock national news anchor as authoritative. They prefer different voices, especially their own. Thus, it could be said that dialogue is the language of the millennial generation.

Take note of this fact. A sermon without dialogue will not reach millennials as effectively as one shaped by it. Why? Because dialogue is the language of millennials. Therefore, dialogical preaching is what they will best respond to. The tone and tenor of dialogue differ significantly from monologue. We cannot approach preaching, in the study or in the pulpit, as a monologue speaking at the millennial congregation. The effective preacher will engage in a respectful dialogue, thinking out loud with the millennial congregation. Think of some of the preachers you see winning with people between twenty-five and forty years old (as of the time of this writing). You may think it is because they are closer to their age—and they may be—but that proximity only gives the preacher the benefit of learning their language intuitively. Even if we are further apart in age, we can learn another language if we want to.

I was amazed to discover the significant Hispanic population that lives within five miles of the church I serve. Imagine if we wanted to grow our congregation by reaching that nearby Hispanic community. What must we do to overcome the language and cultural barriers? It might be wise to develop a relationship with someone in that community and support them as they lead their people. But how would I develop that relationship? If I were fluent in Spanish, it would make the whole situation a lot easier, but I do not know much Spanish. My hope would be that they knew English. Or I might purchase Rosetta Stone. Or I could enroll in a course to learn Spanish. The point is that something strategic would have to be done to get through the language barrier. Whatever it would cost would be worth it because my aim would be to help our church serve that Hispanic community.

I was also amazed to discover the growing sense of disconnect between people of different generations in our church. So, after hosting the focus groups and discovering the themes they revealed, I shared them with our entire congregation. It was insightful to see how each generation felt alienated by the others. We were all disarmed by sharing the needs, desires, and perspectives of each group openly. The experience brought unity and a sigh of relief. Parents and children felt they better understood each other. I felt like we were a step closer to really becoming the kind of intergenerational church Jesus desires. The costs of conducting focus groups, transcribing the manuscripts, and scouring them for insight was well worth it. Whatever it costs to ensure we serve the elders, boomers, Gen Xers, millennials, Gen Zers, and beyond is worth it.

Language Is More

As the youngest of four children, Journee knows that she cannot force her older brothers to do anything. She also knows that being the only girl works in her favor with their dad. So, before she tries to force her brother out of her favorite spot on the couch, she runs to Dad. She hops into his lap. "Daddy, Jaxson is sitting in my favorite spot," she whines. "It's my favorite spot because it's next to your seat and I can see better from there," she explains before Dad can respond. "Tell Jaxson that Daddy says to move over." After giving her dad a kiss, she jumps down and scurries into the family room. "Jaxson, Daddy said to move over so that I can sit there please," she says. Jaxson, though frustrated, moves anyway. Journee sits down and smiles.

Even at six years old, Journee is a master of reasoning and rhetoric. Her reasoning was sound. She was right to know she could not make her brother move. Her rhetoric moved her dad to leverage his authority to help her. Then, her use of her dad's authority was all the persuasion her brother needed. Journee thought before speaking, adjusted her approach to each person, and was able to influence action as a result. Preachers can learn a lot from little Journee. She thought about who she was speaking to and how best to persuade them to act. She exemplifies the essence of communicating for effect.

Preaching: Rhetoric and Reasoning

Language is more than words. Language is more than phraseology. Language is most powerful in rhetoric. L. Susan Bond defines rhetoric in the following way: "Rhetoric involves the way oral discourse constructs an argument strategy to persuade not just individuals but groups toward corporate activity."[1] The inherent danger of emphasizing rhetoric and reasoning in preaching is to overemphasize it. Overusing rhetoric drifts into oratorical grandstanding. As preachers we know that rhetorical eloquence must not be primarily for people's pleasure. Eloquence should glorify God by pointing all listeners to the truth about God for the purpose of falling deeper in love with God.

The apostle Paul states his stance on the relationship between preaching and rhetorical eloquence in 1 Corinthians 1:17 where he says, "For Christ did not send me to baptize but to preach the gospel, and not with words of eloquent wisdom, lest the cross of Christ be emptied of its power" (ESV). Paul continues presenting his perspective on the relationship between preaching and rhetorical eloquence in the following chapter.

> I decided to know nothing among you except Jesus Christ and Him crucified. And I was with you in weakness and in fear and much trembling, and my speech and my message were not in plausible words of wisdom, but in demonstration of the Spirit and of power, so that your faith might not rest in the wisdom of men but in the power of God. (1 Cor 2:2-5 ESV)

The reactionary conclusion could be that these passages are anti-rhetoric. However, Paul is not deemphasizing the role of a carefully crafted message. Although this is inspired Scripture, the passage itself was written carefully to persuade its readers. That is rhetoric at work under the authority of the Holy Spirit. Paul is not decrying eloquence but trying to hold the preacher accountable when employing the tools of rhetoric. He is not trying to restrict the preacher from using the tools of rhetoric.

The gospel was the content of Paul's preaching, and his approach was cruciform, meaning the tools of his rhetoric were nailed to the cross, such that rhetoric died to itself and lived only to serve the gospel.[2] Paul's cruciform preaching was less about entertaining an audience with his oratorical skill as it was about the audience experiencing Christ through him. He used rhetoric to exalt Christ. He did not use rhetoric to impress people.

When a herald comes to the city square with a message from the throne, his aim is not primarily to receive applause. Rather, he is focused on relaying the message as it has been spoken from the throne. The herald must, above all things, be faithful and be clear. The goal of a cruciform rhetoric is to be faithful, not fancy; and to be clear, not clever.[3]

Cruciform preaching toward an intergenerational effectiveness is preaching that removes obstacles of understanding for people of all ages. We should use carefully crafted sermons to eliminate obstacles of understanding, not show off our skills. These obstacles are removed by clearing the way rhetorically for the gospel to reach the ears of every hearer. Think about it: People have real, emotional, spiritual, and mental obstacles to trusting the gospel. Preaching is God's chosen medium for advancing the gospel. So, preaching must help move people past their obstacles and toward faith. Rhetoric is intentional persuasion that counteracts the beliefs that reinforce a person's internal obstacles. Therefore, it is not the use of rhetoric that weakens preaching. It is the misuse, abuse, and overuse of rhetorical exhibitionism that weakens preaching. Rhetoric must be used in service of the gospel and the hearer.

Becoming an effective preacher is about understanding language and the people who will hear their language spoken. Language, when used fluently, is understanding. The preacher's understanding of people and their language is clearly heard in the shaping of her rhetoric.

Teachers are great examples for preachers who seek to become intergenerationally effective. They can be certified for different grade levels and subject matters. In developing their lesson plans, teachers have clarity on the intended purpose of every class session. Their effectiveness, however, is in their capacity to adjust how they teach. Great teachers understand that it is not about their preference in presentation, but how the students best learn. Howard Gardner's theory of multiple intelligences is a useful tool in determining the people groups among students.[4]

Interestingly, Gardner's concept of linguistic intelligence encourages communicators seeking to learn the languages of the generations:

> Linguistic intelligence involves sensitivity to spoken and written language, the ability to learn languages, and the capacity to use language to accomplish certain goals. This intelligence includes the ability to effectively use language to express oneself rhetorically or poetically; and language as a means to remember information. Writers, poets, lawyers and speakers are among those that Howard Gardner sees as having high linguistic intelligence.[5]

I have no doubt that preachers are also implied in this list of those who exercise linguistic intelligence. Preachers are users of language. To reach a people group, the preacher must be intentional about speaking the language of that people group. Timothy Keller encourages us to "address different groups directly, showing that you know they are there, as though you are dialoguing with them."[6] Keller's advice for attracting the urbanite holds true for attracting the generations.

The generation that preachers address directly by speaking about their needs, appreciating their formative experiences, and using language they prefer will be present in their congregations. The generation that preachers do not address by ignoring their needs, demonizing their formative experiences, and refusing to learn their language will not be present in their congregations. A millennial preacher's efforts to reach unchurched boomers might mean acknowledging Woodstock. A boomer preacher's efforts to reach unchurched millennials may look like acknowledging Coachella. The primary issue is not about the ethical nature of these music festivals, but the fact that these music festivals are nostalgic because of the generation they influenced. Effective intergenerational preaching seeks to find commonalities between the two festivals, acknowledging their cultural importance, and turning toward the use of music for worshiping Jesus as music's highest potential.

Whoever the preacher can prove she understands will show up and lean into the preaching experience. Whoever the preacher proves she refuses to try to understand will not show up. James Earl Massey says, "Blessed is the preacher who so speaks as to assure all hearers that God knows and loves each one, that even though facing a crowd, God always has the individual in mind."[7] When addressing a crowd, God wants baby boomers to know they are loved. When addressing boomers, God always has each boomer in mind. Effective intergenerational preaching will reflect this reality.

Language is clarifying. Where rhetoric displays understanding of the hearer, reasoning creates clarity for the hearer. Clarity in communication happens best when the communicator reasons with the hearer. Reasoning enables the hearer to make an informed decision about the message. Keller says, "Preaching is compelling . . . if the preachers understand their hearts and culture so well that listeners feel the force of the sermon's reasoning, even if in the end they don't agree with it."[8] This is the feeling a person gets when they offer sentiments like, "It seemed like the preacher was talking directly to me." This result cannot be sustained over time by mistake. The preacher must strategize intentionally for every generation to "feel the force of the sermon's reasoning."

The intentional use of reasoning does not guarantee results in preaching, but it increases the probability of effective preaching. Reasoning does not guarantee the hearer will believe, but it ensures the hearer will understand. Facilitating understanding and providing clarity happens when the preacher knows the purpose of their voice.

The Preacher: A Voice for the Text to the People

The preacher's voice is a servant to the biblical text and its authorial intent. Bond says, "Preachers will frequently find themselves involved in a hermeneutical circle: in conversation with the Bible, with traditional, doctrinal understandings, with the contemporary culture, and with the particular congregation."[9] And in that conversation the preacher gives voice to each. The issue comes with determining how to give an equitable voice to each without giving an equal voice to each. There are many poor examples of a preacher's misuse of voice. To pander to the gathered audience by harping on their collective frustrations without explaining how a biblical text mediates wisdom for their experience is a misuse of voice. Doing so may be effective politicking, but it is ineffective preaching. To entertain an audience with light-hearted jokes and half-baked applications is a misuse of voice. It makes for effective stand-up comedy, but it is ineffective preaching. The voice of the preacher is primarily for the sake of the text and the gospel. Thus, the preacher's work is to study the text and labor to communicate the text to the people. Preaching effectively to the generations cannot happen without being primarily faithful to the biblical text.

Faithful preaching is a key step in effective preaching. Paul Windsor believes "faithful biblical preaching is characterized by five key attributes. It opens the Scriptures, enters society, engages the listener, exposes the preacher, and exalts Christ. . . . Truly biblical preaching—complete preaching—weaves together all five elements."[10] Though faithful preaching weaves all five elements together, the first element is the thread without which the whole tapestry would unravel. Entering society and engaging the listener without opening the Scriptures is not faithful preaching. Exposing the preacher without opening the Scriptures makes the preacher the subject of the sermon. Christ, the living Word, is exalted best when revealed through the written Word.

Preaching the Word faithfully means considering how the content of the text influences the rhetoric of the sermon. Bond says, "If the gospel is related to a content, it is also related to a rhetorical intention."[11] The good news of the gospel is in the content about Jesus, communicated with the rhetorical intention of deliverance for sinners. Passages that contain narratives should be communicated with storytelling; apocalyptic passages, with urgency and hope; and prophetic passages, with sobriety and warning. Faithful preaching captures the authorial intent and genre of the text through the corresponding rhetoric of the preacher. It starts with the text and stays in the text. It then reaches out to the listeners with a hand that guides them from their experience into the text, walks them around in the text, and then guides them lovingly back to their experience with the confidence that they can reenter the fray of their lives with a renewed perspective. That is the impact of faithful preaching.

Effective preaching is the goal of faithful preaching. Daniel Overdorf says in *Applying the Sermon*, "Effective preaching, stated simply, has an effect. It makes a difference. It changes hearts. It influences decisions. It equips servants. It spurs obedience. Effective preaching unleashes the Word, not only to inform, but also to transform."[12] Preaching can be faithful to the biblical text without being effective at reaching the heart of the listeners. The complexity of the congregation's demographics makes it increasingly difficult to be effective, especially when it comes to the generational complexities.

It is possible for a chef to faithfully prepare chicken. Monitoring the temperature that the chicken is stored at to protect against salmonella, seasoning it, and cooking it to the desired internal temperature is all faithfulness in cooking chicken. Faithfulness to the cooking process is priority. But right after that is done a chef wants to plate and serve it effectively. How does a chef know they have been effective? If the plate comes back licked clean. Plating the food is key because people eat with their eyes long before they dare to taste the food.

Rhetorical intentionality is the plating of the biblical message to get the gospel past the cultural defenses in the mind of the listener. When preaching to a group of Generation X the text must be plated in an intellectual sermon. Preaching to Gen Xers about the crucifixion of Jesus is faithful. Preaching to them about how crucifixion impacts its victim's body is effective. Preaching to Gen Xers about the resurrection of Jesus is faithful. Preaching to them about how extrabiblical historians captured the beliefs of followers of Jesus from the first century is effective. For Generation X the intellect must be engaged.

Overdorf adds, "Effective preachers connect biblical truth with the questions, struggles, and needs of contemporary listeners."[13] Studying the people without knowing the text is unfaithful preaching. Studying the text without knowing the listener is ineffective preaching. Faithful and effective preaching conjoin the two goals. Faithful and effective preaching is executed in sermon delivery, but it starts with sermon development.

Preparing with a Generational and Life Stage Grid

To preach effectively to an intergenerational congregation, the preacher must prepare with an understanding of each generation and their life stages. Understanding the generations as distinct people groups will increase the preacher's generational intelligence. Understanding the life stage each generation is in will increase the preacher's insight into its current broad range of needs. Haddon Robinson advocates for the use of people grouping, by generation, in conversation with life stage needs to help the preacher become more effective. He says,

> I think it is a good thing for a pastor to make a grid of his congregation. Make the grid any way that you want it, but on the one side put down different age groupings in your church—the boomers, the busters, the millennials. Then come across the other side and have single living with parents, married with no children, married and divorced.

You can have a number of those grids. Then look at those grids and say, "If what I am saying today is God's truth, and I believe it is, how would it apply to a young person who is 18, living at home single? Does it have anything to say to the young woman who is out in the business world and living with a roommate?" If I have that grid when I look at those boxes, things will come to mind, and I will say, "Yeah, if that person was sitting in my office and they said to me, 'How do you cope with a difficult roommate, or how do you handle the frustration of having a boss that is always on your back?'" Does this text have anything to say to that person? Sometimes you say, yes it does. So, it enables you to think of your audience—to take them more seriously because you can see individuals or groups of individuals more clearly.[14]

Check out the example of a generational and life stage grid that I have designed.[15]

Generational people group	Generational span	Current age range	Current life stages
Traditionalists/ Elders/Silent	before 1945	74+	Seniors (70+)
Baby boomers	1946–1964	55–73	Seniors (70+) Second adulthood (55–69)
Generation X	1965–1982	40–54	Adulthood (30–54)
Millennials	1983–1998	20–39	Adulthood (30–54) Emerging adulthood (24–29)
Generation Z	1999–present	19 & under	Young adulthood (18–23) Adolescence (13–17) Childhood (2–12) Infancy (0–2)

Figure 3.1. Generational and life stage grid (as of 2022)

Please take this and use it. This is a key tool to add to your sermon preparation process. When you look at the grid, it is important to note that while the generational people groups are static, the life stages are dynamic. Baby boomers will always be baby boomers but have not always been in the second adulthood[16] life stage. Second adulthood is the gap of time between adulthood and senior years. Those in second adulthood are old enough to have retired from a career, raised a family, or given more than two decades to public service. They are also young enough to take on a second career. They are old enough to have a pension plan but too young to draw from it or social security.

The generational cultures continue to evolve as generations grow older, moving out of and into different life stages. Thus, it is vital that whatever grid the preacher designs is updated at least once annually for data accuracy. Perhaps a retreat for you and your team of ministers would give you a chance to update the grid accordingly as you develop the annual preaching plan.

The goal is to diversify whom we picture as we prepare. It is highly likely that whomever we envision most as we prepare will become the ones present as we preach. Likewise, whichever group we envision least when we prepare will become the ones absent as we are preaching. How many preachers deliberately envision an intergenerational audience? If I can envision an interethnic congregation and see them show up on Sunday, so can I envision an intergenerational audience and experience the same results. They show up and log on because we speak to the audience we envision. "If you speak to them, they will come," has replaced "if you build it, they will come."

4

Good News for Elders

The generation born before 1945 has been called "Builders" by some and "Traditionalists" by others. We will call them the elders—not to be confused with church elders. Many were born in the Roaring Twenties, some in the '30s and early '40s, and all came of age during the Great Depression and World War II. That should tell you a lot about them as a people group. Surviving the worst economic downturn in American history instilled a deep appreciation for every little bit. It birthed in them a work ethic that may have not yet been duplicated in the generations that followed. They are steadfast, resourceful, and often stoic.

African Americans were the viable minority in the 1920s, '30s, and '40s. Their experience was rife with conflict, far more so than their White counterparts. Black men were sent to fight on the front lines for a country that scarcely recognized their humanity when they returned home. Black women, particularly in the South, were hardened by the burden of caring for children and managing fieldwork. Other Blacks migrated to the North and Midwest, moving to big cities. This great migration (1916–1970) catalyzed the Harlem Renaissance (1910–1935). Black culture distinguished itself from American culture. Racism evolved into various forms, and whether in the Jim Crow South or the Industrial North, Black Americans were not treated with civil equality.

For women, the beginning of the elder generation was marked by international movements for women's rights, first with the suffragists, then increasing access to education, jobs, and economic influence. While one may debate our nation's progress in gender equality since then, the girls and youth who grew up in the elder generation experienced a steep change in both opportunity and responsibility within their lifetime. This cohort of women went to work in droves. While men were away fighting in the war, women were home fighting for the economy and providing for their families. Though not given equal pay for equal qualifications and work, the elders began a trend of women working outside the home, especially in cities. This created tension with women of more traditional values and may have become the seed that led to the rise of feminism in the next generation. Women also were given the right to vote when the Nineteenth Amendment was ratified in 1920. This freedom for women to express themselves politically and vocationally led to the freedom for them to express themselves fashionably. The elders developed a distinct fashion in the '20s that their great grands have gladly (and perhaps unknowingly) adopted today.

Two key tech advancements changed America in the '20s: radios and cars. We will focus primarily on radios because they are a medium of communication. What homes used to wait to read in the newspaper, now they could hear on the radio. Live broadcasts gripped America and served to create a sense of shared experience that impacted culture. Radio stations started to pop up alongside radios in homes. The one-way dynamic of communication via radio is key to understanding the language of the elders. Many elders heard Franklin D. Roosevelt's words about a "date which will live in infamy," via radio. This generation was led by the only American president to serve almost four terms during the country's worst economic downturn and a global war. Their reverence for FDR is telltale of their respect for leadership. It is also key to understanding their generational language.

Current Stats on Elders

	Born . . .	Age range (in 2022)	Population in 2022*	States with highest %**
Elders	before 1945	77+	approx. **6%** of US adult population	Maine Florida West Virginia

* based on Barna definitions of birth years of this generation; among 18+ population
** www.census.gov/newsroom/press-releases/2020/65-older-population-grows.html and
www.governing.com/archive/gov-generational-population-data-maps-by-state.html

Fig 4.1. Current stats on elders

One of the defining factors of this generation is their affiliation with Christianity—or at least espousal of Christian moral values—and the degree to which the church influences their life and perspective. Since the youngest of this generation are in their late-seventies and many face physical barriers to attending church consistently, we will look at the statistics[1] for this generation from a decade prior, starting at 2011 and going back to 1991. In 2011, elders would have been ages sixty-five and older, and in 1991, forty-five and older. Thus, some of the change may be due to the impact of health challenges and physical infirmities on their habits.

In 2011, more than seven out of ten elders (71 percent) had been to a regular church service in the past six months, a group

Racial Identity
(multiple selections allowed)

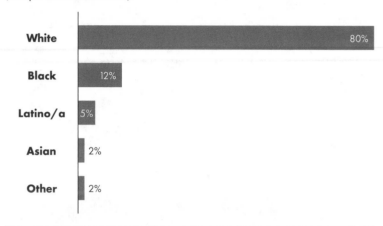

Religious Identity

Relationship Status

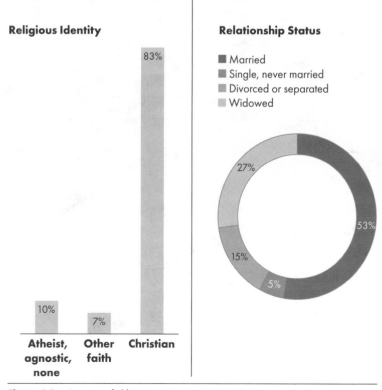

Figure 4.2a. A portrait of elders

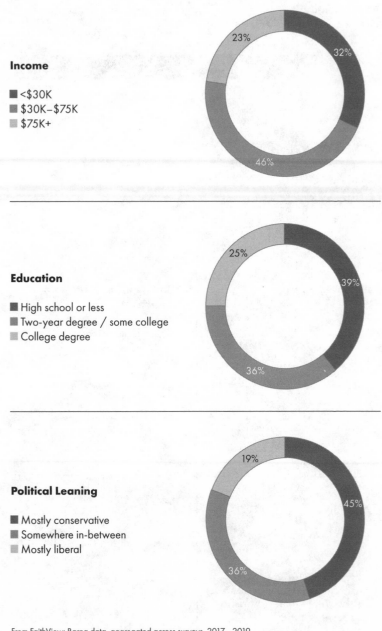

Income

- ■ <$30K
- ■ $30K–$75K
- ■ $75K+

32%
23%
46%

Education

- ■ High school or less
- ■ Two-year degree / some college
- ■ College degree

39%
25%
36%

Political Leaning

- ■ Mostly conservative
- ■ Somewhere in-between
- ■ Mostly liberal

45%
19%
36%

From FaithView: Barna data, aggregated across surveys, 2017–2019.

Figure 4.2b. A portrait of elders

Barna would call "churched." That number was eight out of ten in 1991. That same percentage of elders expressed belief that "God is the all-knowing, all-powerful creator of the universe who continues to rule that world today"—Barna's definition of an orthodox view of God. A similar proportion says they have made a personal commitment to Jesus in their life. All these stats come together to paint a picture that this is, by far, the most churched and Christianized generation in America today. In fact, in a recent study, nine out of ten elders who are currently "unchurched" said they did attend church in their teens. Because most elders have roots in the church, Christianity defined the culture of their day, and even unchurched elders are familiar with the basics of Christianity and church.

Key Insights on Elders' Preferences

Despite their long-time connection to the church, as they age and face physical and mental deterioration, many elders begin to lose their connection to their church. They may not be able to attend regularly. Many of their friends have passed away or moved to places where they can receive ongoing care. Pastors who shepherded them for years may have moved on or retired. All these circumstances, plus a realization that they are the outliers of their church by age, could leave our seniors with a sense of disconnection from their church community. In our survey, elders were least likely to strongly agree that they feel connected to and included in their church community. They also were unlikely to agree that their church intentionally engages people like themselves.

% who agree strongly . . .

■ Feel connected and included in church community
■ Church intentionally engages people like me

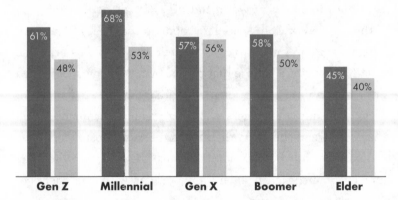

Respondents who "agree strongly" that, prior to Covid-19, their church community connected well with them.
n = 513 churchgoers, research conducted by Barna Group | December 18, 2020–January 20, 2021.

Figure 4.3. Churchgoers' sense of connection with their church

When it comes to preaching, elders are squarely focused on application. From a list of potential outcomes from a sermon, six out of ten say it should be applicable to their life. This means that what they are taught from the Bible should be able to be put into practice in their lives. This is substantially more important to them than gaining a greater, deeper understanding of a passage or experiencing a connection to God—their second and third choices. Elders respond well to clarity in life instruction, relating both to the way they prefer to take in information (direct and clear) and what they value (Christian morals and lifestyle, reflecting their upbringing).

Most Essential Outcomes of a
Christian Sermon (Top 3)[2]

■ I find it applicable to my life   60%

■ I understand a passage in greater detail
than I did before   36%

■ I felt a personal connection to God   28%

Regarding sermon styles, elders show a bit more variety. The example elder-style preachers tested with this group included Billy Graham, famed international evangelist, and Floyd H. Flake, pastor of Greater Allen AME Cathedral in New York. Slightly less than half of churched adults (41 percent) selected these audio excerpts as their favorite, while significantly more (61 percent) of unchurched elders selected these preachers. For this group, which does not regularly sit under the preaching of a local church, such classic styles of preaching resonate.

Propositional Preaching—
The Language of Elders

I would define the language of the elders as "propositional." Elders prefer propositional language, especially from an authoritative voice. Their preference was shaped, in large part, by speeches via radio. Propositional communication has more answers than questions. It is certain, firm, and rousing. Propositional communication tells you what it is about to say, then says it. There is no turning to the right or the left.

I encourage you to start with a cursory observation of the types of preachers both born in and able to reach people within the elder generation. Some of the greatest preachers of the twentieth century preached propositionally. The cultural, historical, and sociological reasons for elders preferring propositional preaching includes, but may not be limited to, more of a folk knowledge than an extensive formal education, slower movement of information, limited mediums of communication, and a high view of spiritual leaders and church. Because many people born before 1946 did not achieve high levels of education, simpler language and rhetoric are more appealing.

However, elders are not unintelligent. They possess a wisdom gained from struggle through some of America's worse times. For the believing group of elders, the faithfulness of God through those events need not be questioned in preaching. Furthermore, the high view of spiritual leaders and church meant less doubt in their messages and less need for argumentation. Preachers like Billy Graham, Floyd Flake, Dr. Charles Stanley, and Dr. Tony Evans, all of whom preach propositionally, appeal greatly to the elders. Graham, Flake, and Stanley are elders, so they preach in their native generational tongue. Evans is a boomer. However, Evans is one of the older boomers, being born in 1949, and likely grew up listening to propositional preaching.

Good News in the Elder's Native Tongue

Have you heard Rev. S. M. Lockridge's sermon "That's My King"? If so, it epitomizes propositional preaching in its sure, authoritative, and steadily rousing tone. Here is my own example of how to preach the gospel propositionally. I encourage you to read this in a sure, authoritative, and steadily rising tone.

Jesus is the only Savior. John 3:16 says in the KJV, "For God so loved the world, that he gave his only begotten Son, that whosoever believeth in him should not perish, but have everlasting life." Let me be clear. When I say Jesus is the Savior, I am not saying that the church is a savior. The church cannot save anybody! Only Jesus can save. I do not care if it is Baptist, or Methodist, AME, nondenominational, Church of God, Church of God in Christ, megachurch, or a micro church. No church can save. But every church should preach Jesus. And teach Jesus. Because only Jesus saves! When I say Jesus is the only Savior, I am not talking about the preacher. Preachers cannot save. I do not care if the preacher is called "pastor" or "apostle." They can be "overseer," "bishop," or "reverend." There is no title higher than "only begotten Son." Only Jesus offers salvation is my point. That is clear in the Bible.

In the world we live in there are many options, but there is only one choice. And it is your choice to make. John 3:16 says God "gave his only begotten Son, that whosoever believeth in him should not perish" (KJV). But if you do not believe, you choose to perish. The choice is yours. There is one thing God gave everybody in this world that you can control . . . free will. You choose how you will use your free will. The only way to apply John 3:16 to your life is to ask Jesus to be your Savior.

A lot of us live our lives thinking that we are blossoming . . . it's all going well . . . we feel good . . . it must be good. We do not realize that when we do not choose Jesus, we are like a leaf plucked from a tree. The minute you separate from your source of nourishment you begin the process of a slow death. In the beginning it is fun. It is all good because you are still green. Your life might seem beautiful now, things might be looking up for you now, but you are separated from God. God is the life source. Eventually, a life separated from God will start turning brown. Then it will dry out. And if physical death comes, you have waited until it is too late to make your decision. Do not wait. Choose life today! Jesus is the only way to eternal life. That is good news for us! You have lived a long life. You have survived struggles that younger generations may never know. God has been with you. And in Jesus, He promises to always be with us for all eternity! So, choose Jesus today.

Did you notice the propositional nature of that gospel message? It was forceful. It was sure and unflinching. There was no doubt. There were no questions. I used more "you" than "we" language when emphasizing the application of accepting Jesus. There was no consideration of any reasonable alternatives. It was Jesus or nothing at all. Even the analogy of the leaf was intentional to paint a grim picture of the soul when separated from God by sin. It ended with a crescendo of God being good all the time, and for all time. This is merely an example, but it is the essence of propositional preaching. It reassures, strengthens, and gives hope to hearts. The unique fears, needs, and experiences of elders make them fond of propositional preaching, especially when the forceful and authoritative tone brings clarity to stories and doctrines of Scripture.

Gloria, a single, live-in grandmother, loves propositional preaching. She comes to church every week with her Bible and something to take notes with. She listens attentively, as if to sift through the sermon in search for clarity. Straightforward teaching of the Bible is what she prefers and loves. She communicated her appreciation for clear propositional preaching when she said to me, "The sermon was so simple that a child could understand." This is feedback I get often from elders. I am amazed that they acknowledge the desire for childlike clarity. Gloria's refreshing smile and grateful remarks encourage us to practice propositional preaching.

5

Good News for Baby Boomers

The year was 1945. World War II had finally come to an end. Soldiers returned home, and in 1946 the most babies in American history were born. From 1946 to 1964 approximately four million babies were born per year, hence the "boom" in baby boomers. Boomers were the largest generation in American history. The United States had seen the Great Depression and a war, now it celebrated the coos of seventy-six million bundles of joy. The sheer nature of their bigness caused the world to naturally reshape itself around them, their ideas, their leaders, and their buying potential.

In many ways the coming-of-age experience of baby boomers was a tension between longing for the past and pushing forward toward change. And because of their size, boomers played a vocal role in some of this change. The civil rights movement of the late 1950s and 1960s dramatically shifted American society, as did ongoing women's rights initiatives. And while the world enjoyed relative peace following WWII, the United States was still engaged heavily in the Korean and Vietnam Wars, with much backlash against the latter, especially from baby boomers, who were being drafted into a long and seemingly insurmountable conflict.

Watergate made it harder to believe in the US government. Skepticism of religion and its leaders proved that Jim Jones's deadly elixir harmed more than those who drank it. Much of this instability led to a pervasive anti-institutional attitude becoming deeply rooted in baby boomers.

Still today, many distrust government, corporate entities, major media, academic institutions—anything "big," even if they benefit from them (as they now do from social security). Psychologically, these experiences fostered a sense of both entitlement (because of the relative peace many White suburban Americans experienced) and protectionism (because of the change they lived through), rather than the resilience and collectivism more commonly ex-hibited by their parents. And in some ways, their values were passed down to their kids, the millennials, and younger Gen Xers of today.

After WWII, African American soldiers returned home to a seg-regated America. Their families boomed with babies too. However, many raised their families in small living quarters of the rural South or crowded tenements of the North. The pride Blacks had in the Tuskegee Airmen was matched only by the distrust they had of the government for the Tuskegee Experiment. To understand that crossroad is to understand the America that Black boomers grew up in. Young Black boomers were infused with the musical sounds of Stevie Wonder and Michael Jackson. They were also inspired by the activism of Rev. Dr. Martin Luther King Jr. and Malcolm X. Their childhoods and teen years were marred though by the assassina-tions of these leaders, not to mention the communal trauma expe-rienced following the deaths of Emmett Till and Medgar Evers. Even with the legal integration of schools, it is no wonder why the Black community grew more suspicious of their own nation. Black baby boomers all have a shared and unique experience within the events that occurred during their coming-of-age years.

Women growing up in the baby boomer generation sprung from the shoulders of their mothers. They continued to both experience greater opportunity and wrestle with the role of women in society. In many ways they were given unprecedented access (just one example is the female human "computers" who helped launch the NASA space missions), yet many were conflicted and clung to traditional values (think June Cleaver in *Leave It to Beaver* or Margaret Anderson in *Father Knows Best*). A portion of female baby boomers took the mantle from their mothers and championed women's rights in the form of personal agency (including healthcare, fertility rights, and no-fault divorce) and vocational opportunity, breaking glass ceilings in academia, the corporate world, arts and literature, and civic leadership. Others pursued a quiet, happy life and retreated to what became the American suburbs. These are two extremes of the portrait of boomer women, but they are meant to illustrate the dichotomy that grew as their worldviews formed and were shaped by the moment of transition in which they became adults.

Current Stats on Boomers

	Born . . .	Age range (in 2022)	Population in 2022*	States with highest %**
Baby boomers	1946–1964	58–76	approx. **30%** of US adult population	Arizona Florida Nevada

* based on Barna definitions of birth years of this generation; among 18+ population
** www.census.gov/newsroom/press-releases/2020/65-older-population-grows.html and
    www.governing.com/archive/gov-generational-population-data-maps-by-state.html

Figure 5.1. Current stats on boomers

Like their parents, baby boomers grew up in a society defined by Christian values and norms, but primarily in their youngest

Racial Identity
(multiple selections allowed)

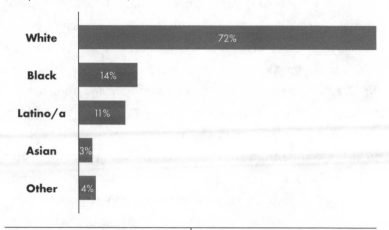

White	72%
Black	14%
Latino/a	11%
Asian	3%
Other	4%

Religious Identity

Relationship Status

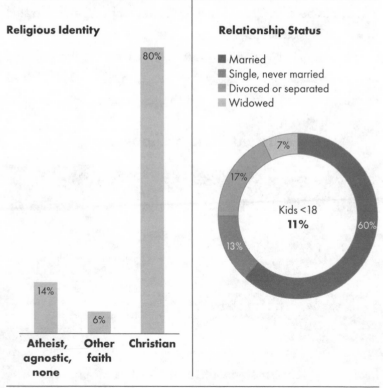

- Married
- Single, never married
- Divorced or separated
- Widowed

Religious Identity:
- Atheist, agnostic, none: 14%
- Other faith: 6%
- Christian: 80%

Relationship Status:
- 60%
- 13%
- 17%
- 7%

Kids <18
11%

Figure 5.2a. A portrait of boomers

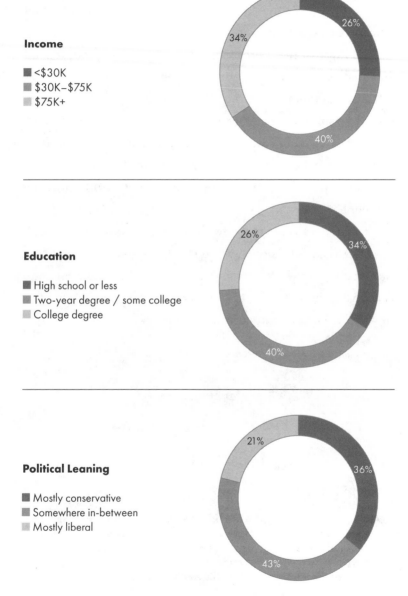

Income

- <$30K
- $30K–$75K
- $75K+

26%

34%

40%

Education

- High school or less
- Two-year degree / some college
- College degree

26%

34%

40%

Political Leaning

- Mostly conservative
- Somewhere in-between
- Mostly liberal

21%

36%

43%

From FaithView: Barna data, aggregated across surveys, 2017–2019.

Figure 5.2b. A portrait of boomers

years. Upon reaching young adulthood, many boomers went in one of three spiritual directions: post-modernism or other human-centered worldviews spawned by modern enlightenment; backlash against the church fueled by legitimate gripes or general anti-institutionalism; or entrenchment in Christianity, very often of the moralistic nature. If these three directions sound overly pessimistic, they may be. The church at large remained influential in many ways, and baby boomers did not fully abandon churches or the Christian faith. Yet Barna data shows that seeds planted in this generation came to fruition in the subsequent cohorts.

This 2017 study of practicing Christians—those who consider their faith important and attend church regularly—shows how the postmodern worldview is even present in the church. There is a small group of older Christians who hold these views, and these seeds blossom into a sizable minority in younger adults.

% who agree strongly . . .

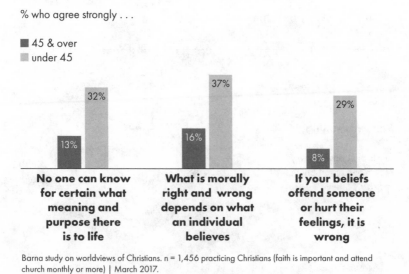

Barna study on worldviews of Christians. n = 1,456 practicing Christians (faith is important and attend church monthly or more) | March 2017.

Figure 5.3. Postmodern beliefs among practicing Christians

Research on the broader population of baby boomers, which Barna has tracked over time, shows a steady decline among the generation in church engagement:

- In 1991 (when boomers were in the family stage of life in their 30s to 50s), half attended church weekly.

- In 2011 (boomers were in their 50s to 70s), that number dropped to 38 percent, while more than 41 percent were completely unchurched (had not attended a church in the past six months or more).

- By 2019 (before the Covid-19 pandemic), just 33 percent of boomers came to church weekly, and half were unchurched.

As with elders, it is reasonable to assume that in the past decade, much of the drop-off may be due to declining health or mobility. However, the decline from thirty years ago suggests a realigning of priorities that does not include church for many boomers. Additionally, a look at their underlying beliefs suggests an eroding of the Christian belief system they grew up in. By 2019, only 61 percent of boomers affirmed an orthodox belief in God (believing that God is the omniscient, omnipotent Creator of the universe who still rules the world today), and just 57 percent agree that the Bible is accurate in all its teachings. For those within the church, boomers are often in positions of leadership and authority and/or provide substantial financial backing to the church's important work. They are essential cornerstones of the body of Christ. At the same time, Barna studies continue to uncover weakened engagement among this generation—at church and at home. A picture of isolation appears as these Christians have moved from work into retirement and turned their focus to enjoying life more than to establishing new habits of community and relational commitment.

Key Insights on Boomers' Preferences

We see these same dynamics defining boomers' engagement with their church. Though they mostly feel connected and included, only half agree that their church reaches out to them. As a result, their connectedness erodes over time.

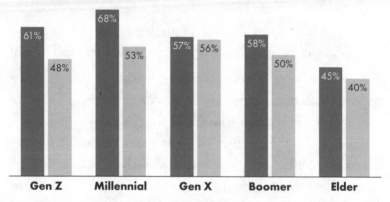

% who agree strongly . . .

■ Feel connected and included in church community
■ Church intentionally engages people like me

	Gen Z	Millennial	Gen X	Boomer	Elder
Feel connected and included in church community	61%	68%	57%	58%	45%
Church intentionally engages people like me	48%	53%	56%	50%	40%

Respondents who "agree strongly" that, prior to Covid-19, their church community connected well with them. n = 513 churchgoers, research conducted by Barna Group | December 18, 2020–January 20, 2021.

Figure 5.4. Churchgoers' sense of connection with their church

If boomers are feeling less engaged, it is important that they connect with the teaching. What a baby boomer desires when it comes to preaching is most commonly application to their life (50 percent). One-third say the most essential outcome is feeling a personal connection with God, and just over one-quarter have a sense of encouragement when a sermon leaves them with a better understanding of a passage.

Most Essential Outcomes of a
Christian Sermon (Top 3)[1]

■ I find it applicable to my life   50%

■ I felt a personal connection to God   34%

■ I understand a passage in greater detail
   than I did before   28%

When it comes to sermon styles boomers express a range of preferences. In our research, we asked churchgoers and non-churchgoers to listen to several audio excerpts from sermons. One was from a preacher that typically aimed their message to their generation, and another that tended to appeal to a different generation. Our two baby boomer examples were Robert Smith Jr. and Charles Stanley. Slightly less than half of churched adults (41 percent) preferred these preachers, while only 33 percent of unchurched adults selected these. Other selections were spread across the example preachers.

Skeptical Preaching—
The Language of Boomers

Boomers are diverse in their preferences for preaching. However, based on the historic dynamics that shaped their generation, I would define the language of the boomers as "skeptical." Though they enjoy propositional preaching, boomers represent the moving of the hearer from purely propositional toward something more conversational. Boomers are more on the propositional end of the spectrum, but not as squarely propositional as their parents. Skeptical preaching teases out tension before it ends with a proposition. Boomers enjoy the thrill of the sermonic tension, especially when it ends with a clear and applicable resolution.

The baby boomer generation diverged from their parents in many ways. Boomers moved to cities, received post-secondary educations, were employed as professionals, and lived by the motto of "do your own thing." Thus, boomers were more likely to ask questions and diverge from their parents' way of doing things. Cultural phenomena like Woodstock and The Isley Brothers' "It's Your Thing" are microcosms of the boomers' skepticism. Boomers may desire more tension in preaching than that offered in purely propositional preaching. C. S. Lewis's trilemma in *Mere Christianity* may epitomize the appetite for a hint of skepticism before returning to accepting a proposition. Preachers like Dr. Gardner C. Taylor and Dr. Robert Smith Jr. preach with palpable tension and have great appeal to the boomers. Taylor was born in 1918 and therefore a member of the elder generation. Smith was born in the early '50s, so he is a boomer. Both are so highly educated and skilled oratorically that they could easily appeal to elders, boomers, and Gen X. But Taylor's preaching ministry soared during the boomers' coming of age, and Smith is adept at preaching in his native generational tongue. Joyce Meyer's preaching appeals to the boomers' desire for clear application in their preaching. It is no wonder then why she has been able to fill arenas for years. Joyce was born at the tail end of the elder generation but came of age with boomers.

Good News in the Boomer's Native Tongue

Here is an example of how to preach the gospel skeptically. I encourage you to read this in a teasing and edgy tone that slowly becomes surer and clearer.

I have good news for you: Jesus is the Savior. But some of you may be wondering, "Is Jesus really the only savior?" The Bible tells us that the answer is yes. John 3:16 says in the NKJV, "For God so loved the world that He gave His only begotten Son, that whoever believes in Him should not perish but have everlasting life." When we read John's verse, we see that God gave his only begotten Son. The word we may assume we understand is the word son. *When we hear the phrase "Son of God," we think "Daddy and child." Especially if we are Westerners. In Western culture daddies and children have a similarity in likeness but a clear rank in position. There is no equality in authority. When ancient Jews hear "son of" they think "equal to." This is totally different. So, when Jesus accepted the title "Son of God," his contemporaries felt like that was blasphemy. To say that Jesus was the Son of God would mean he was equal to God. But was he really?*

A couple of times we see in the Scripture how Jesus implies his identity. Maybe you remember this story in Exodus 3. Moses is minding his business on the mountain, and he sees a bush that is on fire but not burning up. Moses goes over to the bush to see what is going on. A voice from inside the bush says, "Take off your shoes," and then the voice says, "Tell Pharaoh to let my people go." So, Moses looks and says, "Who should I tell Pharaoh this is coming from?" And the voice from the bush says, "Tell him that I AM sent you." That is Exodus 3. Now consider John 8:58. Jesus said, "Before Abraham was . . . I am." When we read that we may not understand it, but if you were one of the Jews that Jesus was talking to that would be offensive.

First, because Abraham is the father of faith, nobody was greater than him. No one was more important in the Jewish community. So, for Jews to see this thirty-something-year-old man claiming he was bigger and better than Abraham was not okay. Not only did he say before Abraham I existed, but he also said before Abraham was, and then he signed a blank check—"I am." In saying "I am," Jesus was intentionally drawing their attention back to Moses' bush experience. Jesus implies in John 8:58 that he is God and therefore existed before their fathers and faith leaders. So, his audience was offended and wanted to crucify him. They killed him for charges of blasphemy. The distinguishing fact though is that he rose in three days. When he rose, he had all power in his hands.

It is based on that resurrection that we can remove all doubt about the identity of Jesus! He is God's only Son. He is God in the flesh. He is risen. He offers salvation to you today!

This is an example of skeptical preaching. There is a tinge of doubt. The hearer can sit in a bit of tension before rushing to a resolution. However, it ends in a sure resolution.

Lena is a boomer. Born in the rural South, she has lived in New Jersey, Georgia, and the Carolinas. As the second of eleven, a mother of two, grandmother of four, and great grandmother of three, she seeks to be a godly example to her family. She loves preaching that helps her think and often says, "I have read that passage before but have never thought about it in this way." She appreciates being able to explore the Scriptures, listen to different perspectives, and land on the truth. Skeptical preaching, as has been defined and exemplified, helps her to continue to grow in her knowledge of God and the Bible.

6

Good News for Generation X

What else would follow the largest generation in American history, except America's smallest generation? Generation X is composed of those born from 1965 to 1983. This generation came of age with experiences that pushed their skepticism toward cynicism. As the first generation of "latch-key kids," they learned not to count on others. Not on their parents. Not on those in authority. Not on social security or pensions. Gen Xers were influenced by many acts of betrayal from people they trusted. They learned to count on themselves, to make their own destiny, and once they got a taste of the economic boom of the 1980s, they were motivated and driven to succeed.

Xers are instinctively distrusting and require evidentiary proof before they will believe anything. Who could blame them? They believed their parents would be married forever, then experienced the highest divorce rate in recent history. Many of them developed distrust in religion on the heels of Jim Bakker's fraudulent activities. Some Xers wanted to be astronauts, until the Challenger disaster. The Gulf War waged in the Middle East was one thing, but the Oklahoma City bombing and the Columbine massacre hit very close to home.

However, there was one positive influence on Xers that had a tremendous impact on the way they respond to communication: the technological advancements of personal computers forever changed Xers and the world. Many of them remember life before the internet and even the first time they received an email. Couple those tech advancements with many of them being the first in their families to receive college degrees, and what you have is the most intellectual generation America had seen at that time. Their doubt of institutions would only be eclipsed by their expectation to be convinced with evidence.

African American Gen Xers fall right into these experiences, except they were uniquely shaped by distinctly racial events. In addition to the layers of distrust already mentioned in their families, church, and government, Black Xers have more cause for their reticence to trust. The horrific Atlanta child murders ascribed to Wayne Williams, Rodney King's beating and the subsequent rioting, and mass incarceration left ineffaceable imprints on Black Xers. The events surrounding Williams and King are widely known and can be easily researched. Mass incarceration, on the other hand, is more insidious in its impact on the Black community.

America's war on drugs led to the disproportionate incarceration of Black youth and men. Mass incarceration is used to describe the mathematic phenomenon that 13 percent of the nation's population makes up more than 34 percent of its prison population.[1] Those numbers reflect a reality for Black Xers who watched family members, friends, or even themselves become convicted felons. The residual effect of mass incarceration on the Black community has been detrimental to its families, economy, and potential to thrive. The rise in cults and religious ideals that stimulate the Black intellect is a direct result of the inherent distrust Black Xers have that has been reinforced through tidal waves of systemic racism.

Other ethnic groups gained traction in America during Gen X's coming of age. In the 1970s, four million people immigrated to the United States, then six million in the 1980s, then immigration peaked in the 1990s at eleven million in that decade. While Blacks were going to prison in droves, people from around the world were migrating to America in droves. Others in Gen X attended college and entered the workforce with an increasingly diverse peer group that opened their eyes to global issues and served to spur on their ambition. Gen Xers became ambitious yet remained distrusting.

As with the generations before them, Gen X women continued to advance in their opportunities in education, work, and sports, boosted by Title IX. Female artists, especially in the entertainment industries, began to feature prominently and even lead in defining new styles and trends. Women stepped confidently into leadership roles, power, and influence, chronicled by a plethora of movies and television shows as a cultural affirmation and setting of new norms for "girl power."

Current Stats on Xers

	Born . . .	Age range (in 2022)	Population in 2022*	States with highest %**
Gen X	1965–1983	39–57	approx. **30%** of US adult population	Georgia Nevada Colorado

* based on Barna definitions of birth years of this generation; among 18+ population
** www.census.gov/newsroom/press-releases/2020/65-older-population-grows.html and
www.governing.com/archive/gov-generational-population-data-maps-by-state.html

Figure 6.1. Current stats on Xers

Racial Identity
(multiple selections allowed)

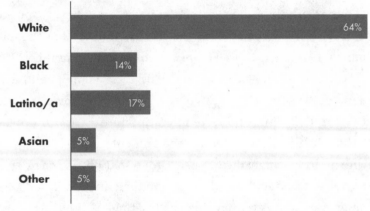

White — 64%
Black — 14%
Latino/a — 17%
Asian — 5%
Other — 5%

Religious Identity

Relationship Status

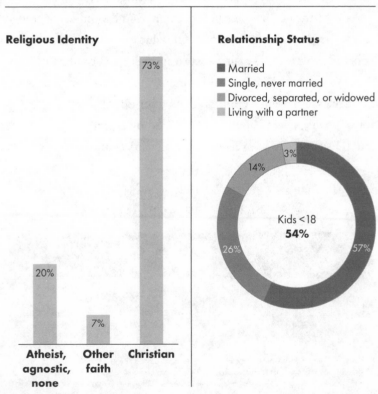

- Married
- Single, never married
- Divorced, separated, or widowed
- Living with a partner

Atheist, agnostic, none — 20%
Other faith — 7%
Christian — 73%

Kids <18
54%

57%
26%
14%
3%

Figure 6.2a. A portrait of Gen X

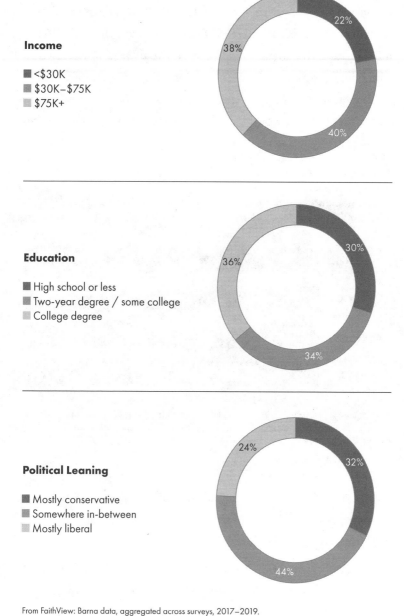

Income

- ■ <$30K
- ■ $30K–$75K
- ■ $75K+

22%

38%

40%

Education

- ■ High school or less
- ■ Two-year degree / some college
- ■ College degree

30%

36%

34%

Political Leaning

- ■ Mostly conservative
- ■ Somewhere in-between
- ■ Mostly liberal

24%

32%

44%

From FaithView: Barna data, aggregated across surveys, 2017–2019.

Figure 6.2b. A portrait of Gen X

Spiritually, the pendulum swung in both directions for Gen X. While adoption of postmodern and secular worldviews continued to gather speed, many in Gen X fully embraced spirituality. A significant minority championed "new spirituality," characterized as a mix between astrology, mysticism, and Eastern religious beliefs.

Many Gen Xers began to perceive a tension or even conflict between the Bible and science, and their veneration of science as the ultimate truth influences Christian and non-Christian worldviews.

■ In **Conflict** - I consider myself on the side of **science**
■ **Independent** - They refer to different aspects of reality
■ **Complementary** - Each can be used to help support the other
■ In **Conflict** - I consider myself on the side of the **Bible**

Boomer	16%	25%	45%	13%
Gen X	19%	30%	36%	15%
Millennial	26%	30%	25%	19%
Gen Z	24%	31%	28%	17%

Barna Group study: Gen Z | n = 1,490 US teens 13–18 & n = 1,517 adults 19+, November 4–16, 2016.

Figure 6.3. "Science and the Bible are . . ."

At the same time, the church experienced a resurgence, fueled by the rise of megachurches and the proliferation of parachurch ministries. Together these forces accounted for an uptick in Christian engagement during Gen X's formative years:

- ■ In 1991 (when Gen X was in their teens and 20s), 71 percent self-identified as Christian, and about half (48 percent) of all Gen Xers said they had made a personal commitment to Jesus Christ.

■ By 2011, when Gen X was in the family and early empty nester stage of life, both numbers rose to 80 percent self-identifying as Christian and 60 percent espousing a faith in Jesus.

■ By 2019 (before the COVID-19 pandemic), affiliation with Christianity had dropped back to 73 percent, but 64 percent claimed a commitment to Christ. Additionally, half of Gen X is churched (attended in past six months).

Key Insights on Xers Preferences

Gen X is "in the middle" when it comes to connectedness and engagement with their church.

% who agree strongly . . .

■ Feel connected and included in church community
▓ Church intentionally engages people like me

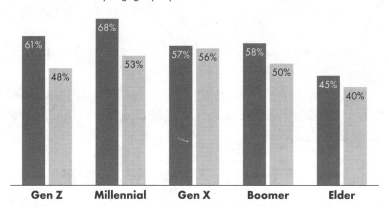

	Gen Z	Millennial	Gen X	Boomer	Elder
Feel connected and included in church community	61%	68%	57%	58%	45%
Church intentionally engages people like me	48%	53%	56%	50%	40%

Respondents who "agree strongly" that, prior to Covid-19, their church community connected well with them. n = 513 churchgoers, research conducted by Barna Group | December 18, 2020–January 20, 2021.

Figure 6.4. Churchgoers' sense of connection with their church

They are also "middle of the road" in terms of their expectations from a sermon. Half desire connection with God, half are looking for life lessons, and all other outcomes fall much further down the list.

Most Essential Outcomes
of a Christian Sermon (Top 2)[2]

▪ I felt a personal connection to God   46%

▪ I find it applicable to my life   46%

They are the most likely, out of all the generations, to leave a service feeling encouraged and inspired (86 percent say they do most of the time). When it comes to sermon *styles* Gen X is very predictable. They lean toward intellectual stimulation . . . which leads them to a personal connection with God and life application. In our research, we asked churchgoers and non-churchgoers to listen to several audio excerpts from sermons. One was from a preacher that typically aimed their message to their generation, and another tended to appeal to a different generation. Our two Gen X examples were Ralph D. West Sr. and Tim Keller. Two-thirds (69 percent) of churched adults preferred these preachers, while 56 percent of unchurched Gen Xers selected them.

Further, when shown an excerpt from the sermon introduction below, Gen Xers most frequently highlighted phrases related to intellect, including "intellectually dishonest," "brains in the car," "check out," and "need to investigate," as wording they connected with in the message.

Intellectual Preaching — The Language of Xers

I define the language of Generation X as "intellectual." Xers will likely consider propositions that can be proven. The requirement to accept any spiritual claims without evidentiary proof sounds too much like what made Bakker possible. Before Xers, the preacher had the benefit of being one of, if not the only, most educated persons in their congregation. Xers began to level the playing field of education. The pew became as smart as and possibly smarter than their preacher. Intellect in the Xers is not a negative. It became the defense mechanism to protect the heart of Xers from being broken yet again. If any generation understands brokenness, it is Generation X. Broken families. Broken homes. Broken relationships. Broken lives. For Xers, their brains stand guard against threats to their hearts and their opportunity. The preacher who desires to be effective with them must appreciate this fact.

As the "show me" generation, Xers are a goad in the backsides of intellectually lazy communicators. No longer is it acceptable just to know what the Bible says. Now the preacher must know what archaeologists, sociologists, and geologists have to say about what the Bible claims. Theology may be the "Queen of the Sciences," but Xers will not bow to her without the presence of other sciences in regalia in her royal court.

In his *Introduction to the Practice of African American Preaching*, Frank Thomas differentiates between folk preaching and educated preaching. He describes each and gives examples of preachers who fit into each category. It could be said that Xers are repulsed by folk preaching. However, they flock to educated, or intellectual preaching. Preachers that reach Xers well have definite components of intellect in their preaching. The intellect is not subtle; it is blatantly apparent. Intellectual preaching is marked by profound research, distinct vernacular, and organized thoughts. Xers are attracted to preachers who are scholars. The preacher must exemplify their brainpower and homework in obvious ways. Xers are also attracted to preachers who speak eloquently. The vocabulary of preachers who reach Xers is usually extensive and filled with multisyllable words that roll off their tongues with phonetic mastery.

Xers are also attracted to preachers whose sermons have a definite structure. The rise in sophisticated outlines and mnemonic devices (e.g., alliteration, acrostics, acronyms, etc.) is the pulpit's response to Xers demanding a sermon that sounds more Socratic than it does sporadic. Preachers like Dr. Carolyn Knight, Dr. Joel Gregory, Dr. Teresa Fry Brown, and Dr. Craig Oliver Sr. are just a few who reach Xers effortlessly. It is no mistake that they all have academic credentials. However, preaching does not have to be heavily academic or purely scholastic to be intellectual. A preacher like Priscilla Shirer (who is academically credentialed), born within Gen X, is a master of intellectual preaching. The clarity of her diction coupled with premium oratorical abilities are factors of intellectual preaching.

Good News in the Xer's Native Tongue

Here is an example of how to preach the gospel intellectually. I encourage you to read this in a tone that is proving a point.

I have good news for Generation X. This news is anchored in proof that Jesus is the Savior. This is not all the proof in the world. This is just some proof for the sake of this point. John 3:16 is saying, God came into the world as a human being through his Son. Other verses in Scripture help us know that historically this person had a name, and his name was Jesus. Jesus, as a historical figure, did in fact walk this earth. Jesus was just as real as anybody else in history that we read about. The question is: how do we know he is truly who he said he was? I invite you to be the judge.

Before a judge can make a verdict, they will need to see two primary factors. First, they will need to hear from witnesses. Second, they will need evidence. Why? Because when the crime took place, the judge was not there to see the crime. But the judge must decide about something they did not personally experience. For the sake of their decision, they have at their disposal witnesses and evidence. And if the witnesses all seem to agree and if the evidence all seems to add up then the judge will have to determine if someone is innocent or guilty as charged. This is all based on witnesses and evidence.

Some of us may ask, "How can I trust Jesus? I was not here to see him." Some of you were not here to see Malcolm X either but you believe he existed. You never even questioned it. You were not here to see Mother Teresa either, but I do not see anyone second-guessing her existence. You were not here to see Abraham Lincoln sign the Emancipation Proclamation, but his signature on that document is evidence that Lincoln existed. Harriet Tubman gets no pushback. If you are Black and your family is from north of the Mason Dixon line, that's evidence that Harriet Tubman existed.

With Jesus, we have an issue. Why though? It is because Jesus is the only one that we are going to have to answer about in eternity. He is the only one who seems to make us upset. We automatically believe in everyone else's existence. When it comes to Jesus, who are the witnesses? Scripture is full of witnesses. But what about the evidence? Most of the time when we use evidence to prove Jesus' existence, we always look at evidence in the Bible. And for many that can be an intellectual issue because the question is whether anybody talked about him outside the Bible. Let me give you three quotes from people outside the Bible. None of these quotes come from religious books. These are not religious people trying to convince you to believe anything. These are nonbelievers mocking the Christian faith.

Tacitus mentions Jesus in his annals—"Consequently, to get rid of the report, Nero fastened the guilt and inflicted the most exquisite tortures on a class hated for their abominations, called Christians by the populace. Christus . . . suffered the extreme penalty during the reign of Tiberius at the hands of one of our procurators, Pontius Pilatus."[3] Lucian, a satirist, said, "The Christians, you know, worship a man to this day—the distinguished personage who introduced their novel rites, and was crucified on that account . . . You see, these misguided creatures start with the general conviction that they are immortal for all time, which explains the contempt of death and voluntary self-devotion which are so common among them."[4] Josephus, author of The Antiquities of the Jews, is considered the greatest Jewish historian. In his book he wrote,

> *Now there was about this time Jesus, a wise man; if it be lawful to call him a man. For he was a doer of wonderful works; a teacher of such men as receive the truth with pleasure. He drew over to him both many of the Jews, and many of the Gentiles. He was [the] Christ. And when Pilate, at the suggestion of the principal men among us, had condemned him to the cross; those that loved him at the first did not forsake him. For he appeared to them alive again, the third day: as the divine prophets had foretold these and ten thousand other wonderful things concerning him. And the tribe of Christians, so named from him, are not extinct at this day.*[5]

We have a regular Greek historian writing about Jesus. He asserts that Nero really does not like this group called Christians. He is just speaking historical facts. Then Lucian . . . He is roasting Christians. He is thinking, These fools are crazy. These writings are not trying to force you to follow Jesus. These are books of people proving the fact that a real man named Jesus lived. So, my question is this: If we can intellectually accept that Jesus walked on earth from reading Tacitus, Lucian, and Josephus, why can't we believe what Matthew, Mark, Luke, and John have to say about Jesus? No truly intellectual person can deny that a man named Jesus lived. You would sound foolish because every historian believed that he lived. Time itself centers around the occasion of his birth. BC and AD have Jesus as its hinge. We know he at least lived! So, if he at least lived, then we are closer to being able to appreciate that he did some things the Bible said he did, which means he might have been the Savior.

Jesus said in John 5:39, "You search the Scriptures because you think they give you eternal life. But the Scriptures point to me!" (NLT). All these words point you to him. If you want to read about Jesus, turn to Genesis. If you open your eyes and bring your heart to the Scriptures when you read, you will see it is all about him. The Gospels tell us about his birth. The Gospels tell us about his childhood. The Gospels tell us about his family. Scripture relays his teachings. The Gospels tell us about his baptism. The Gospels tell us about his miracles. The Gospels tell us about his death, burial, and resurrection. A medical doctor named Luke even tells us that he ascended and that one of these days he is going to return.

The scientific method might help us here. I know some of us have been out of school for years but track with me. The scientific method is how scientists test a hypothesis. It starts with a question, then you do some research, form a hypothesis, experiment on the hypothesis, gather the data and results, and then communicate the data and results. The scientific method is how we start with questions that become laws. To this day nobody will doubt that gravity is a law because the scientific method has proven over and again that if I drop something, it will not fall up. Gravity is a law that dictates how we all live. No one in here will willingly jump out of a plane without a parachute. Our life choices are influenced by this scientific law. Everybody in here is somewhere different in your use of the scientific method regarding Jesus. I champion intellectual honesty. Go ahead and do your own research on Jesus. Go ahead and gather your own data and experiment. I do not mean experiment on what other people might tell you he has done for them. Implement something in your life that he commands and see what happens.

I am glad that to be a believer does not mean I have to become intellectually dishonest. Believers do not have to leave their brains in the car to come to church. That is good news for Generation X, because the need to investigate does not equate to an absence of faith. It might be the necessary cause for a real, deep, and sturdy belief. A belief in the one who can heal all hurts and mend all brokenness.

One main thing this example lacks that is a hallmark of intellectual preaching is a clear outline. I have been taught by a pastor and influenced by many preachers who are masters of intellectual preaching. This type of preaching creates aha moments as it unlocks the brain to be a part of the preaching experience.

7

Good News for Millennials

nterestingly, the smallest generation, Gen X, is sandwiched between the former largest generation, boomers, and the current
largest generation, millennials. Bearing this in mind, it is no
wonder that marketers seemed to skip from appealing to boomers
to trying to sell millennials. Conversations and dialogues around
trends also skipped, seemingly, straight to millennials. Millennials
have the most live births in American history and the most current
living members of any other generation. Born between 1984 and
1998, the millennial generation spans just one-and-a-half decades
compared to other, smaller generations spanning close to
two decades.

How would you describe the communicative palate of a generation made up of the offspring of boomers and Gen Xers? Considered by many as entitled, these boomerang children were reared
by helicopter parents and doting grandparents. Celebrated for
minor achievements, given their heart's desire as children, and
having the world literally at their fingertips has shaped the culture
of the millennial generation. Unfortunately, it is often those
casting blame on the millennial culture who share that blame for
building its foundation. Likely, millennials were given what their

parents never had at the expense of being taught what their parents never knew. It is also likely that the hyperconsumerism of boomers and the latent distrust of Gen Xers has produced in millennials a search for something more satisfying to the soul. This quest for soul satisfaction makes millennials at once more in touch emotionally and more noncommittal vocationally. It is no wonder then why boomer and Gen Xer doorkeepers of industry are put off by what they perceive as entitlement. Older and younger generations have clashed since the beginning of time. But having four living adult generations with one living generation of children, and another one being born now, has complicated the cultural interaction between the generations today.

Cultural clashes between the generations play out on various social front lines. Millennials differ from their parents and grandparents on key issues like job/career choices, marriage, financial management, politics, and spirituality. Chances are you have clashed with someone you love of a different generation over one of the above issues. It happens in homes and in the house of God, in government and in media. On every mountain of culture and crevice of society, generations are misunderstanding each other.

It is not in millennial culture to acquiesce, especially about something they take seriously. If you have ever encountered a millennial refusing to give in to how things are, the problem may not be with them but with the absence of mutual understanding. The goal of intergenerational relatability is not to coerce acceptance of preexisting structures and beliefs. It is not to win the fight. The goal should be understanding, even if we disagree, with an aim at winning the people group. I hope I do not sound defensive, but hey, I am a millennial.

Millennial culture has been shaped by social media, a robust internet, and post-secondary educational opportunities with insurmountable school debt. The attacks of 9/11, the housing bubble burst and subsequent recession, and the election of the first Black president and Black female vice president in US history have impacted us. I can recall sitting in my tenth-grade French class as I watched the planes fly into the World Trade Center towers. The news came over the intercom and our teacher turned on the TV in time for us to see the second tower hit. I was stunned. I did not have the emotional maturity to wrap my head around what I was watching. The fear, doubts, and terror I felt were only matched as I watched the bombing that started the Iraq war. I was more accustomed to schools being shot up than troops being deployed. And for the next two decades of my life, I saw more of both than I care to reflect on. I felt a burden entering the voting booth to elect a president for the first time, a responsibility that brought hope as I have now seen a man and woman of color occupy the presidency and vice presidency. Where Gen Xers are inherently cynical, millennials are relentlessly hopeful. We are hopeful in ourselves and in what we can accomplish together.

Millennials have a different reality than previous generations. Our reality is also a virtual one. We cannot describe millennials without also discussing social media. From Black Planet to Facebook, Vine to TikTok, Pinterest to Instagram, Twitter to Clubhouse, millennials have lived their entire adult lives on social media platforms, shaped by intangible connections no generation before has ever experienced. Social media has leveled many playing fields, especially in business and communication. Millennials can compete as fledgling entrepreneurs because of electronic storefronts. They do not gather around the radio or sit in front of the TV to hear professional news anchors report on the events of the day. They go to their social media platforms and freely offer unsolicited reflections on every topic. Millennials do not accept the ideas of subject matter experts alone; they fancy themselves qualified to share their ideas too. Other generations do not have to agree with this reality, but they must understand it to increase effective communication.

As the most degreed generation in America, and with access to the internet on their phones, millennials are smarter and savvier in their coming-of-age years than any generation that preceded them. The possession of, or access to, so much knowledge can be a cause of much distress when trying to relate to older generations. Millennials may disdain older generations' lack of openness to knowledge. Older generations may be distressed by the millennial tendency toward overconfidence, considering a lack of comparative life experiences. These are major keys to understanding the language of millennials.

Not only are they connected to knowledge of issues and facts, but millennials are also connected to knowledge of the world. One might argue they are the first truly connected generation, where the global spread of culture happens at lightning speed due to social and mainstream media along with connections between in-dividuals. It is possible for a twenty-something in Nebraska to play a video game live with a counterpart in Japan and develop a genuine friendship, enabled by technology. Therefore, millennials are a truly global generation. Because generations come about due to the cultural and geopolitical forces that shape them during their most impressionable years, generations are typically distinct by country. They have different characteristics and include different birth years. But millennials cross that cultural chasm, enabled by technology, to create more of a shared culture than ever before in world history.

For Black and female Americans, the early aughts shattered cul-tural molds. The election of Barack Obama in 2008 was the direct result of many millennials voting for the first time. His election signified real possibilities for Black millennials that were mere dreams for their parents. The politics he ran on and the policies that linger from his eight years as commander in chief are not what matter most to Black millennials. Honestly, many of them disagree on his policies and presidential legacy, but his election was cataclysmic. The same is true for women with the candidacy of Hillary Clinton and the vice presidency of Kamala Harris. The token equality given to women in the '20s has become more of a reality for millennials.

Women can now argue that the greatest athlete, and without question the greatest tennis player, in history is a Black female. Serena Williams won a major tennis tournament while pregnant, a feat a man will never be able to accomplish. Women can also find courage to be financially free in Oprah or to be intellectually equal in Michelle Obama. The alliance of compassionate men for feminist causes has shone a bright light on unequal pay based on gender. Millennial women watched these developments unfold before they turned forty years old.

Current Stats on Millennials

	Born . . .	Age range (in 2022)	Population in 2022*	States with highest %**
Millennials	1984–1998	24–38	approx. **27%** of US adult population	Washington DC Utah Texas

* based on Barna definitions of birth years of this generation; among 18+ population
** www.census.gov/newsroom/press-releases/2020/65-older-population-grows.html and
    www.governing.com/archive/gov-generational-population-data-maps-by-state.html

Figure 7.1. Current stats on millennials

Racial Identity
(multiple selections allowed)

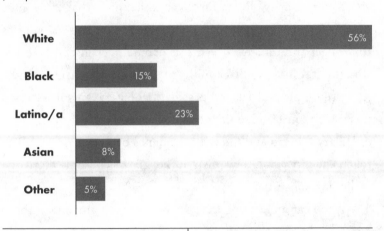

White	56%
Black	15%
Latino/a	23%
Asian	8%
Other	5%

Religious Identity

Relationship Status

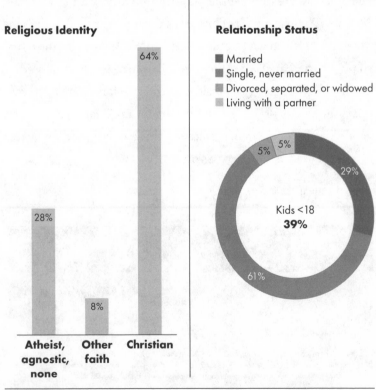

- Married
- Single, never married
- Divorced, separated, or widowed
- Living with a partner

Figure 7.2a. A portrait of millennials

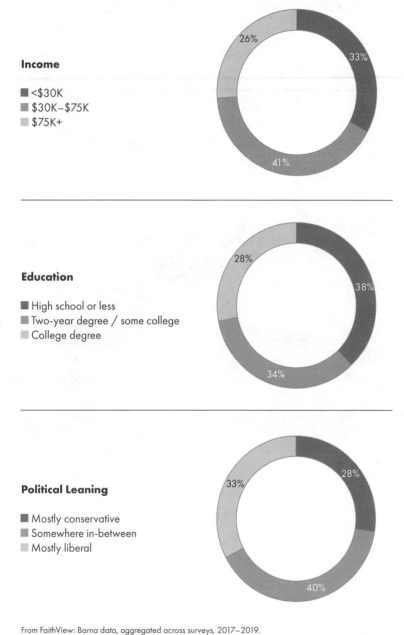

Income

- <$30K
- $30K–$75K
- $75K+

26%
33%
41%

Education

- High school or less
- Two-year degree / some college
- College degree

28%
38%
34%

Political Leaning

- Mostly conservative
- Somewhere in-between
- Mostly liberal

33%
28%
40%

From FaithView: Barna data, aggregated across surveys, 2017–2019.

Figure 7.2b. A portrait of millennials

In 2019, Barna conducted a study with participants between the ages of eighteen and thirty-five (the approximate ages of millennials at the time) in twenty-five countries around the world called *The Connected Generation*. The research aimed to understand the millennial generation's perspectives on spiritual and religious subjects, faith practices, aspirations, relationships, perceptions of leaders, and overall mental and emotional health. What analysts found is that young adults around the globe are often more alike than people of different ages in their own country.

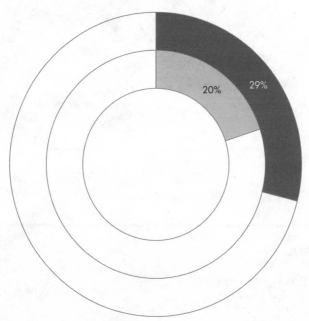

Barna Group study: The Connected Generation. n = 15,369 adults ages 18–35 in 25 countries, including 2,000 in the United States | December 4, 2018–February 15, 2019.

* Anxiety defined as "often feeling" at least three of these emotions: "anxious about important decisions," "sad or depressed," "insecure in who I am," or "afraid to fail."

Figure 7.3. Incidence of anxiety* in millennials

They report a high engagement with events and occurrences around the globe, but this connected generation feels the impact of broad, global trends more than they feel loved and supported by people close to them. Globally, two out of ten report frequent feelings of anxiety. In the United States, it is three out of ten.

"I often feel . . ."

■ United States
▨ Global

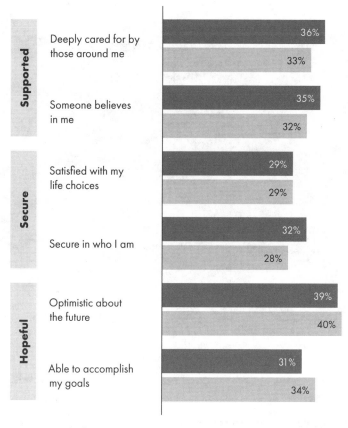

Barna Group study: The Connected Generation. n = 15,369 adults ages 18–35 in 25 countries, including 2,000 in the United States | December 4, 2018–February 15, 2019.

Figure 7.4. Positive emotions among young adults

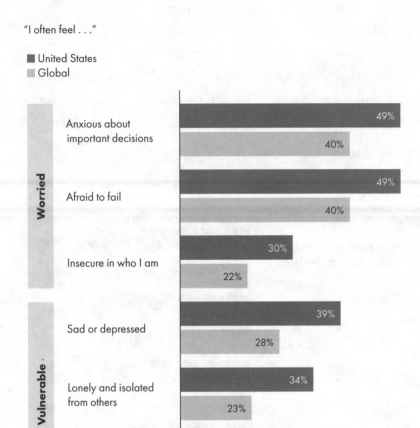

"I often feel . . ."

■ United States
▨ Global

Worried
- Anxious about important decisions — United States 49%, Global 40%
- Afraid to fail — United States 49%, Global 40%
- Insecure in who I am — United States 30%, Global 22%

Vulnerable
- Sad or depressed — United States 39%, Global 28%
- Lonely and isolated from others — United States 34%, Global 23%
- There aren't enough opportunities available to me — United States 26%, Global 23%

Barna Group study: The Connected Generation. n = 15,369 adults ages 18–35 in 25 countries, including 2,000 in the United States | December 4, 2018–February 15, 2019.

Figure 7.5. Negative emotions among young adults

Potentially adding to the anxiety is a perception that certain issues and problems are large or insurmountable. Concerns about corruption are primary in the minds of young adults around the world, but American millennials' next greatest concern is racism, an issue that has only intensified in urgency over the past few

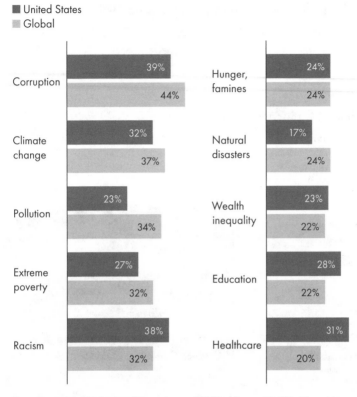

Barna Group study: The Connected Generation. n = 15,369 adults ages 18–35 in 25 countries, including 2,000 in the United States | December 4, 2018–February 15, 2019.

Figure 7.6. Concerns about the world's future

years. Next on the list: climate change, followed by healthcare (pre-pandemic) and education.

Despite feelings of helplessness or anxiety, millennials, and Christians in particular, report a commitment to pursuing justice and generosity. Consistently Barna's research has found those millennials who stick with their Christian faith are committed to living a life in which they "walk the talk" of their beliefs. Nicknamed "the connected generation," millennials do not want to be mere *consumers*; they want to be *contributors*. Being a Christian requires steadfast character for millennials. There are no social pressures to live a moral life of upholding Christian values. Today's millennials are brave in their faith when they have it.

For over a decade Barna has tracked the continual slide of children who grew up in the church, drifted away from church in adulthood, and for some, even away from faith. In *Faith for Exiles*, authors David Kinnaman and Mark Matlock found that more than

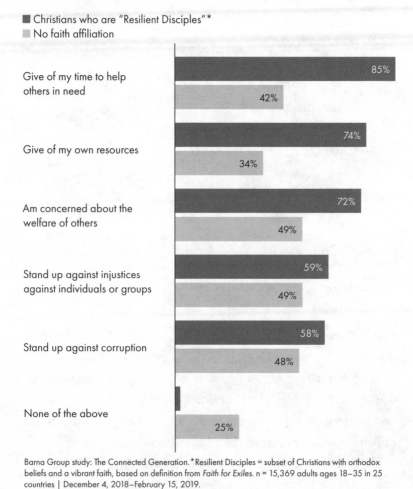

■ Christians who are "Resilient Disciples"*
■ No faith affiliation

Give of my time to help others in need — 85% / 42%

Give of my own resources — 74% / 34%

Am concerned about the welfare of others — 72% / 49%

Stand up against injustices against individuals or groups — 59% / 49%

Stand up against corruption — 58% / 48%

None of the above — / 25%

Barna Group study: The Connected Generation. *Resilient Disciples = subset of Christians with orthodox beliefs and a vibrant faith, based on definition from *Faith for Exiles*. n = 15,369 adults ages 18–35 in 25 countries | December 4, 2018–February 15, 2019.

Figure 7.7. "Because of my beliefs, it is important that I . . ."

half of 18-to-29-year-olds (millennials) who had grown up in the church walked away in young adulthood. Twenty-two percent no longer call themselves Christian, and three out of ten say they are Christian but do not attend church. At this pace, it is no wonder that a faithful, practicing millennial expresses conviction—few have incentive to stick with their faith. Those who do are serious.

It's in this context that we consider how to communicate with millennials—both inside and outside the church.

Key Insights on Millennials Preferences

Just as millennial Christians express convictions about their faith, many who do have a church home express a strong sense of belonging and connectedness. They are the most likely of any generation to say they feel connected to and included in their church community when they have a church community.

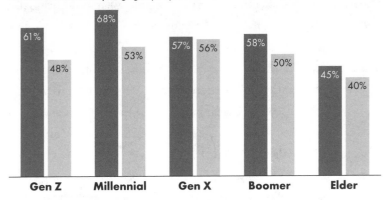

% who agree strongly . . .

■ Feel connected and included in church community
▨ Church intentionally engages people like me

Gen Z: 61%, 48%
Millennial: 68%, 53%
Gen X: 57%, 56%
Boomer: 58%, 50%
Elder: 45%, 40%

Respondents who "agree strongly" that, prior to Covid-19, their church community connected well with them. n = 513 churchgoers, research conducted by Barna Group | December 18, 2020–January 20, 2021.

Figure 7.8. Churchgoers' sense of connection with their church

However, what millennials desire when it comes to preaching varies significantly from person to person. Just over one-third (37 percent) say the most essential outcome of a sermon is feeling a personal connection with God. However, close behind this are life application (34 percent) and a better understanding of a passage (31 percent). Approximately two out of ten gave various other essential outcomes from a sermon. On this point, there is a diversity of opinions and preferences among millennials.

Most Essential Outcomes of a Christian Sermon (Top 3)[1]

■ I felt a personal connection to God — 37%

■ I find it applicable to my life — 34%

■ I understand a passage in greater detail
than I did before — 31%

Unfortunately, about one-third (33 percent) of millennial adults say they walk out of a worship service feeling "belittled" at least half of the time, and a quarter (23 percent) report feeling "lost." These are signs that the sermon is not connecting. Additionally, half of millennials (46 percent) believe that older adults desire "something a little different" than what they themselves desire in a sermon, and another 11 percent say something *very* different. This is significantly higher than what other generations report, showing their disconnect with older generations.

However, those who can master their communication style will engage millennials. In our research, our two millennial examples were Dharius Daniels and Andy Stanley, both of whom appeal to millennials in their message and style. Daniels is a young Gen Xer and Stanley is a boomer. Neither of them is a millennial, but they both connect well with millennials. Of all the generations tested, millennials displayed the strongest preference for these two pastors' messages, with two-thirds of churched as well as unchurched adults selecting these as their most preferred message (66 and 64 percent, respectively). These findings support that not only do these preachers speak the language of millennials, but they also speak the language of this era. The language of millennials is the language of today. Other notable preachers who connect well with millennials are John Mark Comer and Mike Todd.

This research also uncovered that unchurched millennials in particular respond with significant interest to the Gen X–style language of investigation, especially when it is invitational and affirms the millennial listener's intellectual capacity. Gen X's emphasis on intellectually responsible and substantiated truth claims is a phenomenon that continued to grow in the next generation, such that the millennial and Gen Z worldviews are also very much pro-evidence.

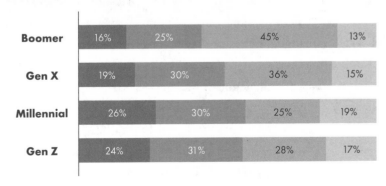

■ In **Conflict** - I consider myself on the side of **science**
■ **Independent** - They refer to different aspects of reality
■ **Complementary** - Each can be used to help support the other
▨ In **Conflict** - I consider myself on the side of the **Bible**

Boomer	16%	25%	45%	13%
Gen X	19%	30%	36%	15%
Millennial	26%	30%	25%	19%
Gen Z	24%	31%	28%	17%

Barna Group study: Gen Z | n = 1,490 US teens 13–18 & n = 1,517 adults 19+, November 4–16, 2016.

Figure 7.9. "Science and the Bible are . . ."

Unchurched millennials frequently selected investigative language from the Gen X version when presented with sermon excerpts in this research: "intellectually dishonest," "brains in the car," "I encourage you to investigate," "study history," "check out archaeological studies," "see what Greek scholars, who were not Christian, had to say about him," "find what many ex-atheists have found," and, most encouragingly, "Jesus really is who the Bible says he is." This is great news from the non-Christian millennials that we preachers all want to connect with! The preference of millennials is in addition to, not in lieu of, the previous generation's preference. This means that if you already preach intellectually, keep doing it. Just add to it the language of millennials.

Dialogical Preaching—
The Language of Millennials

The growth of social media, free access to information, and mold-breaking political events have shaped the language of millennials, which I define as "dialogical." Dialogue is by nature two-way communication that requires mutual amounts of listening and speaking from both parties. Dialogue happens when two people are conversant, open, and arrive together at an unforeseen outcome. Dialogue requires an open mind, open ears, and open heart. In dialogue, neither party guides the other, but both are walking together.

The demand for dialogue by millennials is based primarily on a healthy (maybe even over-confident) sense of self. This self-individuation is usually not tethered to anything external. For example, a twenty-five-year-old millennial can live with a parent rent-free and still assert that they are an adult. Then they could demand dialogue from that parent about lifestyle choices, financial decisions, or spiritual beliefs. Dialogue is not totally foreign to boomers and Gen Xers. The difference is that they will dialogue to a certain point with a person they do not view as a peer. In their minds, their authority is tied to their external status as the bill payer, parent, boss, or their life experience. Therefore, based on that status alone, dialogue should be minimal. Millennials do not see it that way. Remember that the goal is not to agree, but to understand. Millennials, too, must be willing to understand the perspective of boomers and Gen Xers.

If it is difficult to dialogue when a boomer parent and their millennial child are talking, imagine when a preacher is trying to communicate with a group of millennials with whom they have no filial connection! What was already difficult may begin to feel impossible. I want to encourage every seasoned preacher: you can do this. You can expand your tool belt. You can learn to communicate effectively without resorting to cheesy jokes and popular song lyrics. You can learn how to cook it up the way millennials like it. Be encouraged.

Good News in the Millennial's Native Tongue

We cannot claim to love a people group that we refuse to try to understand. Dialogical preaching validates the otherness of its listeners and displays respect for their intellectual independence. Here is an example of how to preach the gospel dialogically. There are other more literal ways to create dialogue by replacing sermons with interviews, but this example is a way to bring the spirit of dialogue into a stand-and-deliver preaching event. I encourage you to read this in a tone that displays listening, creates space for disagreement, and requests an audience to be heard.

There is great news for millennials. To grasp this news, would you consider how Jesus just might be the only Savior? John 3:16 in the New International Version is key for your consideration. "For God so loved the word that he gave his one and only Son." I want to suggest to you that we only have one Savior because God only had one Son. But the reality is this is hard to accept because we live in a world with so many things that promise to save us. Maybe not as explicitly as Jesus does, but implicitly many things offer us salvation. Money promises to save us from poverty. Happiness promises to save us from depression. Likes and loves on social media promise to save us from loneliness. But all of us have tried the above and have discovered that none of them can quite save. Haven't we? We have felt the sting of fat pockets and an impoverished soul. We know the pain of consuming entertainment but never really having joy. And let's not even talk about the ever-widening hole in our soul created by the apparent success of others that we see on social media.

If our decision is not difficult enough already, think of all the different religions in the world that are offered to us. Should we desire something religious, we can find it in a temple or a mosque. We can connect with a church online or offline. We have more options than ever to stimulate spirituality, but they may all seem frivolous. What is the point? The point is this: no wonder Christianity sounds so crazy when we say that Jesus is the only real option in a world full of options. Because every day there are so many things competing for our trust. We live in a world where everything has options. How can a preacher get up and tell you that Jesus is the only way, but McDonald's isn't the only one with a burger? What do you mean the only way? I can get a burger from at least ten different places today. Toyota is not the only car. Is it? So, when we tell people Jesus is the only way, people look at us sideways like, "Hmmm Christians are intolerant." "Christians are judgmental." "Christians don't understand that multiple religions all really preach and teach the same thing." I hear you. Honestly, I feel you too.

It could seem like a stretch, but I want you to consider that Jesus might be the only way to be truly saved. For one, he said he was.

John 14:6, "I am THE way and THE truth." This means that Jesus claimed exclusive rights to being the Savior. But you say, "We live in an age of social media. Pretty much everything we see is a lie. People lie. Just because Jesus said he is the Savior doesn't mean he is." Okay, I hear you, touché. He might not actually be telling the truth from your perspective. But to me what makes Jesus so great is not just that he claimed to be the only Savior. He told those following him in John 2:19, "Look I'm going to show you how powerful I am. Kill me. Go ahead. But be advised that three days after you do, I'm going to get back up again." To "destroy this temple" means to destroy his body. This is called a double-dog dare. Jesus said, "Okay, you want to see who I am? I double-dog dare you, kill me. And in three days—not one or two—in three days, I will rise." Jesus says, "I'm a going to make a fool out of my doubters. I am going to walk on water. I am going to help people. I am going to feed thousands. And they are still going to kill me. And I'm going to come back." That is more than enough information to consider that he might be the only Savior. That is good news for millennials. Because with so many options in this world, it is hard to decipher which one is worthy of any confidence, let alone complete confidence. Jesus, in my opinion, makes a strong case. He does something for us that had never been done before and has never been done since.

The pace and tone of dialogical preaching is marked by a frequent pause for reflection, as if to invite the listener to respond within themselves. What the psalmist would call a *selah*. Dialogical preaching gives the listener time and space to think along with the preacher. The hearers are encouraged to consider the preacher's point because they can hear that the preacher has already honestly considered their point. Though the preacher is guiding the conversation, the preacher is not driving the conversation. The preacher is evidently first a listener. These are the characteristics of effective dialogical preaching.

8

Good News for Generation Z

They began to be born at the turn of the millennium. They are the first generation of the twenty-first century and natives to high tech and social media. Born with iPads in hand and an intuitive knowledge of technology that stumps their parents and grandparents, Generation Z is uniquely positioned to turn the world upside down. The last of Gen Zers are already kindergarteners as I write these words, meaning the eldest of Gen Zers are barely legal adults. Some are college graduates, others are enlisted in the armed services, few are being paid big dollars to play professional sports, and many are building small businesses into recognizable brands. A small but visible minority are eschewing college in pursuit of meaning as social media influencers, professional YouTubers, or tech developers.

Without question the most influential social event on Gen Z will be the global pandemic. There is not a nation, ethnicity, tax bracket, gender, generation, family, or person who experienced the pandemic unscathed. It touched and disrupted the entertainment, travel, and food service industries. Education, government, healthcare, and organized religion were thrust into a new world. It will take years to discover what the pandemic left in its wake. Gen Z will not only be sculpted by it but will likely contend with its effects for the duration of their lives.

Beyond the pandemic, there are unique constraints to the study and understanding of Gen Z. The first is the overwhelming attention given to millennials. All the eyes on millennials have not yet shifted to Gen Zers. This is a constraint in the effort required to understand them as a generation. Our churches are reeling from last-ditch efforts to attract millennials. Meanwhile, Gen Zers may be catching churches off-guard. My hope is to offer some help in connecting with them more effectively.

The second constraint in trying to understand Gen Zers is that most of them are still teens and children. They are mostly in their coming-of-age years now, so their generational proclivities are not yet defined. Furthermore, the type of survey research that Barna Group typically conducts focuses on adults, only capturing the sentiments of the eldest Gen Zers in regular tracking. Gen Z is almost old enough to be more concrete in their perspectives, but many are developing now. This is a constraint—but it could become a significant opportunity. Our churches and communication styles could embrace their needs and reach them before we lose them. Granted, reaching the youngest of them is tethered to reaching their millennial parents, but the opportunity exists. This would require a child-centered agenda, a key factor in an ever-expanding generational intelligence.

The final constraint is the tension between life-stage needs and generational cultures. My belief is that though millennials, Gen Xers, and boomers will all age through life stages, their generational languages will remain intact. Although practical and spiritual needs change based on one's life stage, generational people groups are relatively fixed in their cultural perspectives. Again, one's ability to agree that generations are people groups is necessary to absorb this concept. We often think about people groups through ethnic lenses. Think of White American boomer males. They have specific ethnic perspectives that will remain intact as they age. That is as much a viable statement because of their generation as it is because of their ethnicity. Since Zers are still formulating their generational language, I lean on their life stage needs as a placeholder until more of them complete their coming-of-age years.

When we consider the complexity of our world, it is important to grasp how life stages have adjusted accordingly. Check out these graphs comparing the biblical and modern perspectives of life stages.

Life stage	Age range	Biblical passage / cultural nuance
Infancy	0–2 years old	1 Samuel 1:21-28
Childhood	2–12 years old	Luke 2:41-52
Adulthood	13–59 years old	Bar or bat mitzvah
Elders	60+ years old	Psalm 71:18; Proverbs 16:31; Titus 2:1-3

Figure 8.1a. Biblical times

Life stage	Age range
Infancy	0–2 years old
Childhood	2–12 years old
Adolescence/Teen	12–17 years old
Young adulthood	18–23 years old
Emerging adulthood	24–29 years old
Adulthood	30–54 years old
Second adulthood	55–65 years old
Seniors	65+ years old

Figure 8.1b. Modern times

Even a basic understanding of modern life stages proves that our current world is more complicated socially than the ancient world. Because Gen Zers are just entering young adulthood, their generational tongue is still being developed. Thus, we can conclude two things: First, they will continue the dialogical trend and perhaps go further to the extreme away from the propositional language of elders. Second, we can use relational communication as it connects well with their current life stages. Children listen to people who they trust. From my five years as a youth pastor, I know that this is not so simple with teens and their parents. But as a trusted youth leader, my volunteers and I were able to connect relationally to our teens. You will see echoes of this in the Gen Z data that follows.

Current Stats on Gen Zers

	Born . . .	Age range (in 2022)	Population in 2022*	States with highest %**
Gen Z	1999–2015	7–23	approx. **7%** of US adult population	

* based on Barna definitions of birth years of this generation; among 18+ population
** www.census.gov/newsroom/press-releases/2020/65-older-population-grows.html and www.governing.com/archive/gov-generational-population-data-maps-by-state.html

Figure 8.2. Current stats on Gen Zers

Relationships with older adults are important to Gen Zers, and this is likely due to a blend of their life stage and the generational inclination to prioritize relationships. However, they also tend to say they feel misunderstood.

Racial Identity
(multiple selections allowed)

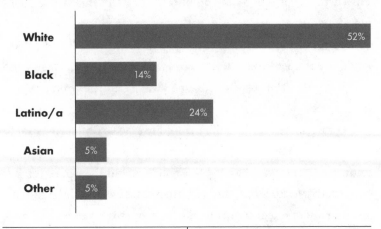

White	52%
Black	14%
Latino/a	24%
Asian	5%
Other	5%

Religious Identity

Relationship Status

- Married
- Single, never married
- Divorced, separated, or widowed
- Living with partner

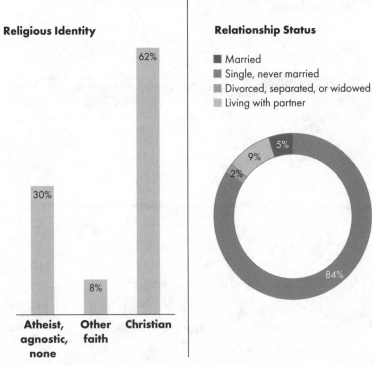

Atheist, agnostic, none — 30%
Other faith — 8%
Christian — 62%

Married 5%
Single, never married 84%
Divorced, separated, or widowed 2%
Living with partner 9%

From FaithView: Barna data, aggregated across surveys, 2017–2019.

Figure 8.3. A portrait of Gen Z

■ Agree strongly
■ Agree somewhat
▨ Disagree somewhat
▨ Disagree strongly

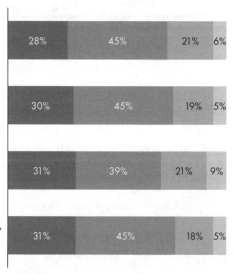

I often look to those who are older than me for advice when I need to make difficult decisions	28%	45%	21% 6%
Those in positions of authority in my life (parents, teachers, etc.) have my best interest in mind	30%	45%	19% 5%
Older people don't seem to understand the pressures my generation is under	31%	39%	21% 9%
I feel valued by the people in my life who are older than me	31%	45%	18% 5%

Barna Group study: Gen Z vol. 2 | n = 1,503 US teens and young adults ages 13–21, June 15–July 17, 2020.

Figure 8.4. Gen Z on intergenerational relationships

Emotionally, Gen Z generally feels free to explore and express their emotions, and often these emotions get the better of them. Gen Z consistently reports feeling a lot of pressure. This often manifests as anxiety or other mental health issues—and it can lead to the use of screens as coping mechanisms.

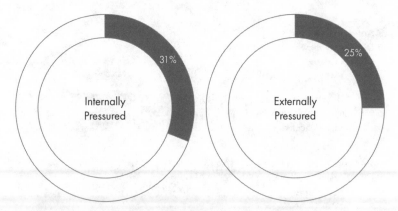

Those who are **internally pressured** always or usually feel
- "pressure to be successful" and
- "a need to be perfect"

Those who are **externally pressured** always or usually feel
- "judged by older generations" and
- "pressured by my parents' expectations"

Barna Group study: Gen Z vol. 2 | n = 1,503 US teens and young adults ages 13–21, June 15–July 17, 2020.

Figure 8.5. Gen Z under pressure

The top negative emotions they report feeling are "tired" (28 percent, a lot of the time; 30 percent, some of the time), followed by "lonely" and "discouraged about the future." Yet despite feelings of caution or discouragement about the future, Gen Z is driven to succeed. They see the possibilities before them and desire to attain certain dreams. Nearly all agree in their hope to achieve a great deal.

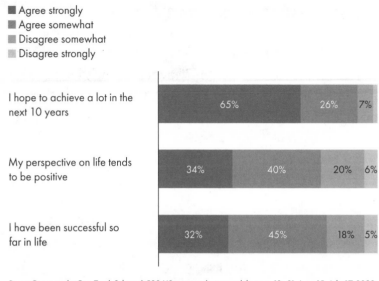

Barna Group study: Gen Z vol. 2 | n = 1,503 US teens and young adults ages 13–21, June 15–July 17, 2020.

Figure 8.6. Gen Z's hope and optimism

In Barna's seminal study on Gen Z conducted in 2016, researchers discovered twice as many Gen Z youth identified as atheist (13 percent) as the generations before them (7 percent for millennials), and fully one-third fell into the non-religious category of atheist, agnostic, or most likely, "none." In its subsequent 2020 study, religious affiliation had not changed, but Barna found that moral relativism and unstable theology had grown over that period. At present 65 percent of Gen Z agree that "many religions can lead to eternal life" (compared with 58 percent in 2016), and one-third (31 percent) strongly agree that what is morally right and wrong changes over time based on what society believes (versus 24 percent in 2016). These data indicate that as Gen Z has moved out into the world as adults, and as they have continually been shaped by societal experiences, they are increasingly adopting a sense of moral relativism.

At the same time, young people of faith—who stand in stark contrast to their peers in their commitment to religious beliefs—continually affirm a desire to live out their faith boldly and missionally. One-third of these Gen Zers agree strongly (and another four in ten agree somewhat) that their faith motivates them to make a difference in the world. In this way they are relatively like millennials. But older generations, take note: the "how" looks different than it does for Christians before them. Gen Zers are motivated to engage in social justice causes at home and abroad, they are concerned about creation care (environmental causes), and many are skeptical of the ethics of traditional mission work. If the experiences of millennials before them are a lesson, church leaders would do well to take these concerns seriously and engage this generation authentically, or risk losing influence with them as they continue to grow.

Key Insights on Gen Zers Preferences

When it comes to their sense of belonging and engagement with their church, Gen Z churchgoers report relatively strong connection. This is somewhat self-fulfilling, as those who do not are apt to quickly leave—especially as they reach adulthood or move off on their own where they are making their own decisions about how and where they invest their time. In 2016, only 43 percent of Gen Z teens and young adults had attended church in the past six months. That number is declining as more in this generation hit adulthood and, even if Christian, find alternative ways to practice their faith.

% who agree strongly . . .

■ Feel connected and included in church community
□ Church intentionally engages people like me

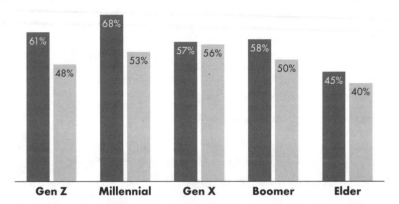

Respondents who "agree strongly" that, prior to Covid-19, their church community connected well with them.
n = 513 churchgoers, research conducted by Barna Group | December 18, 2020–January 20, 2021.

Figure 8.7. Churchgoers' sense of connection with their church

So, what is a Gen Zer looking for when it comes to preaching? Relationship. Half say the most essential outcome of a sermon is feeling a personal connection with God. They are significantly more likely to desire this over life application (32 percent) or a deeper understanding of Scripture (28 percent)—even though these were in their top three—or a personal conviction to change their behavior. Gen Z wants to walk away from a sermon feeling relationally connected.

Most essential outcomes of a Christian sermon (Top 3)[1]

■ I felt a personal connection to God   48%

■ I find it applicable to my life   32%

■ I understand a passage better than I did before   28%

Unfortunately, about two out of ten (23 percent) Gen Z adults say they walk out of a worship service feeling "belittled" at least half of the time, and a similar amount report feeling "lost." These are signs that the sermon is not connecting. Additionally, more than five out of ten (52 percent) Gen Zers believe that older adults need or desire "something a little different" than what they themselves need or desire in a sermon. This is significantly higher than what other generations report, suggesting that they do indeed need a preacher to speak their language.

However, those who can get the relational connection right win the hearts and minds of Gen Z. In our research, our two Gen Z examples were Trip Lee, a Christian rap artist turned preacher who weaves together messages about truth, influence, and creativity; and Judah Smith, a Washington-based pastor whose church is named Churchome for its relational connectivity. Just under half of Gen Z churchgoers as well as non-churchgoers selected these pastors as their most preferred message (46 and 49 percent, respectively). Trip Lee is a millennial and Judah Smith is a Gen Xer. They are proof that preachers can become generationally bilingual.

Additionally, when shown an excerpt from the sermon introduction below, Gen Zers most frequently highlighted relational words, such as describing the "person" of Jesus (or in an alternate sermon, "Daddy and child"), and emotive language, primarily variations of "joy," as the reason they were drawn in by this message.

Relational Preaching— The Language of Gen Zers

The language of Generation Z is relational communication. Data corresponds to this fact. Until they become less abstract and better represented through quantitative tracking, relational communication may have to serve as a placeholder. The simple fact is children and teens will not listen to those who do not relate well to them. The beauty of this relational requirement is that Jesus epitomizes this sort of leadership. Preachers have a real example in our Savior of what it means to be relational with those we disciple. That means the keys to speaking the language of Generation Z fluently has little to do with talking. It is not possible to simply talk relationally; we must be relational. Jesus was accessible, approachable, transparent, gentle, and unrushed. Jesus never acted like he was important, but he always acted like children were important.

The same is true for us, preachers. We will not be able to communicate effectively to Zers if we consider ourselves too important. We cannot be inaccessible, unapproachable, opaque, harsh, and always in a hurry. These qualities may not have counted as much against a preacher in generations past. They may have even worked to keep up the veneer of mysticism. That façade of importance coupled with a palpable charisma has kept many a preacher employed over the decades. Well, not only is it a new millennium, but Gen Zers have ushered in a new day. Charisma does not matter as much to Zers. Being relational does. It is possible to be a charismatic personality without being a relational person. Zers would prefer their preacher be a relational person than a charismatic personality. Barna data shows that the majority of Gen Zers say "older people don't seem to understand the pressures my generation is under" (70 percent agree). We are already lacking a sense of trust. How much more do we need to stop and listen to a highly relational generation that already feels misunderstood? Since many of them are too young to speak for themselves, please accept these ideas on their behalf.

Good News in the Gen Z's Native Tongue

Generation Z is a distinct generational people group with their own developing culture and language. They are children and teens. Their life stages require relational communication. So, here is an example of how to preach the gospel relationally. And of course, one would use simpler words and sentences if they were addressing children. I encourage you to read this in a caring and mutually identifying tone. Think LeVar Burton from *Reading Rainbow* or Mr. Rogers from *Mr. Rogers' Neighborhood*.

I have good news for Generation Z. Jesus would love to be your Savior. How do I know that? Let's look at John 3:16 from the Message Bible. I like how this version words this verse. It says, "This is how much God loved the world: He gave his Son, his one and only Son. And this is why: so that no one need be destroyed; by believing in him, anyone can have a whole and lasting life." That last sentence is where many of our lives revolve every week. All of us in this world want a whole and lasting life, right? You want to be able to say that your life is filled with the deepest joy. So that by the time we get to the end of our days there is no second guessing, there is no regret, and no looking back at time. We want to feel that we did the most that we could with the time that we had. Well, this verse says that type of life is possible. It is possible in this life. It is possible in the life to come after this one. The way toward that type of life happens in a relationship with God. God has established the way to a relationship with him through his Son, Jesus.

The joy of the Christian life is a simple relationship. It is the relationship we have with our Father through his only Son that died for us. Relationships are so critical to many of us that a lot of times we wish we had more friends than we have or better friends than we have. We weep over a broken relationship between loved ones. We are pained by a breakdown among family members. Many of us have experienced the torment of divorce. We have wept as our parents split apart, the whole time fearing we could have done something to help them. So, then it should touch a deep part of our heart, that the primary thing God wants from us is not for us to do something for him but to be something to him. God wants a relationship with us.

When you think of a relationship with God, I do not know what you are thinking. You might see this big controlling God forcing you to do things against your will and taking all the fun out of life. From some examples we have seen, being a believer and being boring just seem to go together. The type of relationship God wants with us is one like my wife has with her mom. Every morning my wife, her mom, and her two sisters are on FaceTime or some type of conference call on speakerphone. Every morning! Whether I am sleeping or awake. They are talking about God knows what! Why? Because they started out as daughters and now that they are grown, they have become friends. That is the same type of relationship God wants with us. God wants us to be his children who mature in our faith and then interact as friends.

Sometimes you could feel like the loner in your family, the outcast of your friends, or that you do not fit in with people you are around. You may ask, "Where do I actually have a group of people I can fit in with?" God says if you want to fit in with me, all it takes is faith. Faith makes you my child. As you mature as my child, we will become friends. Look at what the Bible says in John 1:12, "But to all who believed him and accepted him, he gave the right to become children of God" (NLT). Galatians 4:6 says, "You can tell for sure that you are now fully adopted as his own children because God sent the Spirit of his Son into our lives crying out, 'Papa! Father!'" (MSG). But watch how Jesus expands the picture in John 15. He says, "Greater love has no one than this: to lay down one's life for one's friends" (v. 13). He says, "You are my friends, if you do what I command. I no longer call you servants, because a servant does not know his master's business. Instead, I have called you *friends, for everything that I learned from my Father I have made known to you" (vv. 14-15). That is a powerful picture because it shows us religion was never God's plan; relationship was always God's plan. Religion is fear based. Religion is, "If I don't do this, then God won't do this." Relationship is love based. Relationship says, "I get to do this because of what God has already done." By sending Jesus, the heart of God speaks to us. God says, "I desire to know you, to be known by you." I do not want to be distant from you.*

Perhaps the most heartwarming compliment to my preaching has been when a parent appreciates that their children are receiving the Word. Some Gen Zers speak for themselves, but usually the appreciation comes from a grateful parent. The best way to practical relational preaching is to practice being authentically relational when you are not preaching. Looking to Jesus as the patient, caring, lover of all children, may we reflect his heart for Generation Z, today.

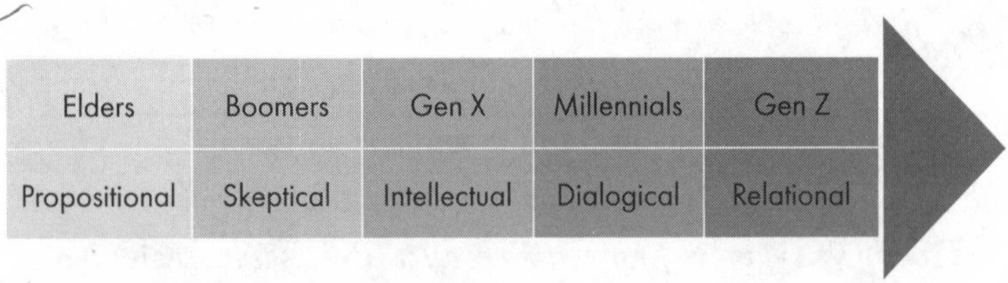

Elders	Boomers	Gen X	Millennials	Gen Z
Propositional	Skeptical	Intellectual	Dialogical	Relational

Figure 8.8. Primary characteristic of effective preaching

The Family of God

Scripture uses multiple metaphors to depict how the church functions. The metaphor of a body might perhaps be the most popular, but the metaphor of a family is the most communal. A body functions through its systems, organs, limbs, and faculties. Seeing the church as a body helps us become more interconnected. A family functions through culture, relationships, roles, intentionality, and love. Seeing the church as a family helps us become more intergenerational.

One of my favorite songs comes from the soundtrack of the stage-play-turned-movie *Dreamgirls*. The musical is a fantastic amalgamation of acting and singing, featuring a fictional female singing group called the Dreamettes, loosely based on the Supremes and other female groups of the 1960s. The story chronicles their early start, discovery, rise to fame, and all the pain interspersed throughout. The lead singer, Effie White, is asked to allow a thinner group member to become the new lead. Her assumption was that she was being discriminated against because of her body image. Being the vocal powerhouse that she was, Effie was incredulous, offended, and suspicious. When given the proposition to step aside to make the group better, she responded with a series of self-interested questions: "What about what I need? What about what's best for me? What about how I feel? What about me?" As a result, she opted to quit the group. For her, it was better to leave altogether than to be repositioned for reasons she did not understand or agree with. In response to her brokenhearted queries her brother, C.C., sang a song called "Family." What he was trying to express to Effie is also true of all Christians. We are family.

Those of us who have placed our eternal confidence in Jesus are spiritual family. Our distinction as Christ-followers supersedes any other demographical distinction we have. Paul is clear in Galatians 3:28 that we are "all one in Christ Jesus." Though our faith in Christ supersedes our other distinctions, it neither eliminates them nor their impact on our experience. I may be a Christ-follower before I am a millennial, but that does not make me less a millennial.

The beauty of the gospel is that it can make us family without making us into each other. Kenyans do not have to become Jews to become Christians. Women do not have to become men to become Christians. People living in poverty do not have to become rich to become Christian. Gen Zers do not have to become baby boomers to become Christian. These demographic distinctions are amoral. They can remain fully intact as we mature in Christ. Again, I say, we are family. It is not just me who says it though, the apostles agree.

"Therefore, as we have opportunity, let us do good to all people, especially to those who belong to the family of believers" (Gal 6:10).

"And in fact, you do love all of God's family throughout Macedonia. Yet we urge you, brothers and sisters, to do so more and more" (1 Thess 4:10).

"Show proper respect to everyone, love the family of believers, fear God, honor the emperor" (1 Pet 2:17).

"Resist him, standing firm in the faith, because you know that the family of believers throughout the world is undergoing the same kind of sufferings" (1 Pet 5:9).

"Both the one who makes people holy and those who are made holy are of the same family. So Jesus is not ashamed to call them brothers and sisters" (Heb 2:11).

From Multigenerational to Intergenerational Churches

To describe a spiritual family as multigenerational is to say it is made up of many generations. To describe it as intergenerational is to say it is a mix of many generations. A mix is composed of ingredients that create a solution of something new together. A multigenerational church functions differently than an intergenerational church. In a multigenerational church, all generations may just be on the same campus or in the same database. A building and a roster do not make up a church family. In an intergenerational church, all generations are equitably nourished, resourced, valued, and growing spiritually. Multigenerational churches can look healthy while suffering the negative impact of generational stratification. Doug Webster says:

> Western culture's generational segregation leads to significant relational fragmentation and disorientation in the household of God. Peter never would have envisioned the church dividing along generational lines, but today it is common to divide along generational lines. This is not a fault of any particular generation, but the multigenerational nature of the household of God is a New Testament expectation.[1]

We want our churches composed of each living generation in a way that all feel seen, loved, and heard. Generational stratification in a multigenerational church looks like a children's ministry over here, something for the teens over there, a gathering for the adults in the main auditorium, and the senior adults in the old sanctuary, but everybody on the board of directors or in senior leadership is all the same generation. The difference in the *multi-* and *inter-* when it comes to generations in the church is not in the programming but in the influencing. How churched is programmed emphasizes the *multi-*. Who uses influence and how people are influenced emphasizes the *inter-*. Communication is a major key to influence. Thus, understanding and using the languages of the generations in church communication improves the intergenerational nature of the family of God.

Honor the Elders but Focus on the Children

Families share more than just a genetic code. Strong families share space, time, and experiences. The Barna Group conducted a study in 2019 called *Households of Faith*, which influenced Don Everts's book *The Spiritually Vibrant Home*. The study found that the members of spiritually vibrant households observed disciplines such as worship and prayer together, had conversations about spiritual topics and Scripture, and practiced hospitality regularly. The same applies to the broader household of the church.

One of the best ways to share space, time, and experiences is over a meal. It is no wonder the first-century church broke bread together to strengthen the familial bond (Acts 2:41-42). Churches today still share meals together, even if it is only a morsel of bread and sip of grape juice in remembrance of the body and blood of Jesus. The spiritual truth behind Holy Communion, despite how different churches practice the ordinance, is that God's table is big enough to extend to any who would pull up a chair in faith. God's table is illimitable. It has many chairs because he has many children.

The application of generational science to the family of God can improve the interconnectedness between the generations. This intergenerational fellowship is an assumption of Paul's (Titus 2). As in biological families, Scripture instructs us to honor the elders and focus on the children. This is a key concept for churches to adopt if they want to become truly intergenerational. Why? Because this value can protect the family of God from the trauma of old generations dying and new generations coming of age. If churches commit to always honoring their seniors, this will ensure the spiritual needs of the elder and boomer generations are met as they age.

Honoring seniors may include a plethora of practical efforts, but it starts with speaking to them in their generational tongue. This is especially important for pastors/preachers who lead people older than them. As millennial pastors, we must do the work of becoming generationally polylingual. Doing so will honor seniors in our preaching, teaching, and leading.

I contend though that the most necessary requirement for the family of God to become truly intergenerational is adopting a child-centered agenda. This will ensure that Gen Z, the alpha generation, and unborn generations will be valued by their spiritual families, resulting in established generations posturing ourselves as lifelong learners of people. How else could we become all things to all people? There is some jarring data that supports the need for a child-centered agenda in intergenerational churches.

In 2019 David Kinnaman, president of Barna Group, published the latest statistics on church dropouts among young adults (between the ages of eighteen and twenty-nine) in his book *Faith for Exiles*. In the eight years since his previous book, *You Lost Me*, the proportion of young adults who were raised in the church and later dropped out rose from 59 percent to 64 percent. Two-thirds of kids raised in the church leave when they reach adulthood. This should be a wake-up call to the church to examine two aspects of ministry: discipling children in their faith and encouraging young adults to remain connected to a church community.

While *Faith for Exiles* points out just how often we drop the baton when attempting to pass faith on from one generation to the next, the primary premise of the book is to understand those who stay—specifically the 10 percent of young adults who were raised in the church and maintain active involvement while expressing a vibrant faith in all aspects of their life. One of the five distinctive characteristics of these "resilient disciples," as Kinnaman and his co-author name them, is *meaningful relationships*. Resilient disciples are significantly more likely than any other child of the church to report "when growing up, I had close personal friends who were adults from my church or faith community." In other words, they experienced *intergenerational discipleship* that led to a unique, lasting faith. What Kinnaman and Barna call meaningful relationships, Kara Powell and Fuller Youth Institute call Keychain Leadership in *Churches Growing Young*, something I experienced in my own life.

My Church Story

The church where I serve as a campus pastor, and have served as youth pastor, is also the church I grew up in from infancy. You might say that I am a prenatal member. Being born and raised in a church I have never left has given me unique perspective. On the one hand my heart hurts as I think of my peers who grew and flew as soon as they could. I also often reflect on the sad reality that many of the youth I pastored also left. On the other hand, I am amazed at how I have been discipled through every stage of my life. I can recall my first Sunday school teacher. I see her face in my head, although she passed when I was thirteen. I can remember lessons I learned singing in choirs, ushering, and serving as a junior deacon. Countless names and faces have shaped me, the two most notable being my youth pastor and senior pastor.

As a teen, I really began to lean into my walk with Christ. I was fully embraced, shepherded, and related to by my youth pastor. In my early twenties, I never could have imagined I would succeed him as the next youth pastor. I felt so honored to do for others what he had done for me. That opportunity came because of a pivotal conversation I had with my pastor as a high school senior. At seventeen years old, I had acknowledged God's call on my life to preach, yet I was looking forward to attending my dream HBCU, and to doing a lot of partying, a little studying, and maybe some growing. I ended up staying home and attending a small Bible college instead. Why? Because my pastor said, "Do not leave for school. Stay home. Stay by my side. I am going to help you. We will be like Paul and Timothy." And that we were. These meaningful relationships gave me several opportunities for keychain leadership over the years. When survivor's remorse threatens to break my heart for my peers and other young people who left church, God's grace gives me hope that helping churches become intergenerational will also mean focusing their agendas on reaching the youngest generations. I believe I am one of many that God will use to help his churches grow healthier as an intergenerational family.

What Was Yours Must Become Ours

The difference between "yours" and "ours" is deeper than simply discarding a letter of the alphabet. The essence of this choice is based on one generation's willingness to open its heart and share with the next. The tension in sharing between generations is the misappropriation of ownership. Whatever God has made the established generation stewards over still, ultimately, belongs to God. God is intergenerational in his workings. He expects the stewards in one generation to intentionally seek out, disciple, and share with stewards of the next. Established generations can share because we were shared with. Even if those before us did not share as they should have, God has certainly overwhelmed every generation of the church with more grace than it deserved. A grace orientation makes it possible to embrace the next generation without fear of loss. Sharing with the next generation is a blessing that reminds us we are family.

Intergenerational
in Everything We Do

The spirit of an organization is more valuable than the slogan it adopts. Southwest Airlines and its cofounder Herb Kelleher are powerful examples of this principle. The way I found out about the spirit of Southwest Airlines was during a family trip to Kentucky. While there, I met a guy who was dating one of my family members. He was in his twenties, probably on the younger side of the millennial generation. We hit it off, except he wanted to spend more time talking about where he worked than anything else. He had not worked at Southwest Airlines for long, but he went on and on about it for hours. He talked to me about his job until I was exhausted listening to him. Then, ironically, his passion struck me and made me lean into the conversation.

The things he raved about had nothing to do with slogans, tag lines, pay scale, or opportunity. He was captivated by the palpable generosity and compassion that oozed through the company. When I began to ask questions, we discovered that Herb Kelleher was the catalyst behind Southwest's culture. Our conversation inspired me so much that I tracked down and read *Forbes* magazine's story on him.[1] People of all ages and life stages benefited from and carried on the spirit of Herb because he embodied what Southwest Airlines represented, and it inspired everything he did as a leader.

The pastor is a leader, administrator, recruiter, mentor, communicator, counselor, and friend. These many invisible hats are worn simultaneously. As we develop messages to nourish the souls of our people, we will do so with knowledge of their unique generational preferences. But our job far exceeds developing and delivering sermons. Preaching, for the pastor, is merely the technical requirement of our overall job. Most of a pastor's role is theoretical, cognitive, and strategic. In addition to feeding souls, pastors are also responsible for leadership, evangelism, discipleship, fellowship, missions, and worship. Embodying an intergenerational culture will influence our preaching as well as the way we carry out the rest of our duties.

Preaching is a unique type of communication. It is God's primary chosen medium to spread the gospel throughout the world and build the church. When it comes to preaching, elders prefer propositional communication, boomers prefer skeptical (toward propositional) communication, Gen X prefers intellectual communication, millennials prefer dialogical communication, and Gen Z prefers relational communication. However, preaching does not have an independent effect. It stimulates the church's culture, theology, leadership, worship, fellowship, discipleship, evangelism, and ministry. These other areas create the health-and-growth results in a church. A commitment to effective intergenerational preaching will influence every area of the church. Let us look at some practical ways this plays out beyond the preaching moment.

Leading Intergenerationally

What truly defines leadership is difficult to pinpoint. How leadership looks may be easier to spot. Therefore, leadership is at once powerful to observe but hard to explain. Many have simply defined it as "influence." I like that definition. That leadership is influence is acceptable. How to exercise that influence is where we all wrestle. For Christian leaders, our unique brand of leadership must be Christlike. It is the type of leadership that exchanges the one for the many. It is service oriented and sacrificially others centered. Christian leadership is not domineering, controlling, manipulative, or power driven, but embraces and embodies the paradoxes of kingdom life. It goes down to be lifted up. It dies to rise again. It gives before it seeks to get. These are sustainable, spiritual, and scriptural principles of leadership that will always be viable.

The leader who seeks to lead an intergenerational church is one who is keenly aware of how the different generations prefer to be influenced. The communication continuum moves from the propositional pole to the relational pole. With each succeeding generation, communicative preferences move further from the propositional and toward the dialogical. Understanding how a group communicates is necessary to developing influence with that group.

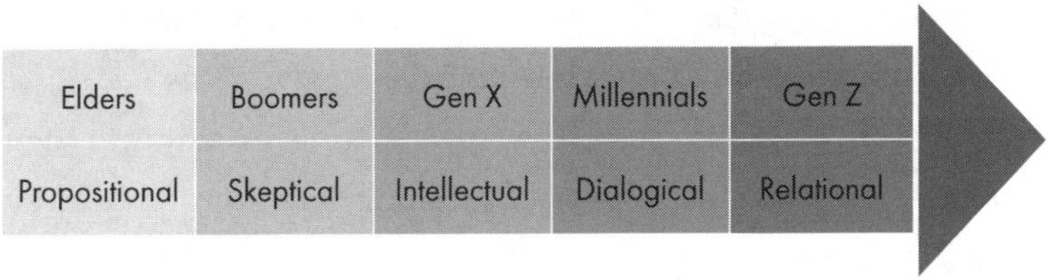

Elders	Boomers	Gen X	Millennials	Gen Z
Propositional	Skeptical	Intellectual	Dialogical	Relational

Figure 10.1. Primary characteristic of effective preaching

With each successive generation, the need for great leadership is reinforced as trust fades. Boomers trust less than elders. Gen X trusts less than boomers. The loss of trust is a direct result of the failure of institutions to uphold their end of the silent agreement with followers. Americans expect politicians to protect the nation from external threats and to improve the quality of life for all its citizens. Children expect their parents to provide for their emotional, physical, and financial needs. Churchgoers expect their pastors to be examples of holy living and to teach the Word without additives. The failures of these institutions have deteriorated trust. Stephen M. R. Covey was right in saying that everything moves at the speed of trust, especially influence.

All people groups have a desire to be led, especially generational groups. Many older and established leaders may accuse younger generations of not wanting to be led, but according to Barna's latest research on trends in the Black church, African American millennials more than any other generation say, "When choosing a church, I very intentionally choose the pastor that I'll be led by" (84 percent agree). The proliferation of celebrity pastors with social media followings in the tens of thousands affirms the universality of this leader preoccupation. The issue for the generations is how they will allow their leaders to influence them.

Jimmy Long highlights the tension with intergenerational leadership in the church. In his book *The Leadership Jump*, he says, "Where existing and emerging leaders are working together, there is a lack of understanding of how to collaborate."[2] A generation's preference in communication may give us some insight into their preference in leadership styles. The millennials' preference for dialogical communication applies to what they expect from established leaders. "Many emerging leaders feel stifled because they come into leadership roles in an existing church, where all the questions of how to organize and how to lead were answered long ago. They do not feel that there is any room or openness for new ways of leading,"[3] says Long, who wrote these words as millennials were bursting on the scene of church leadership.

Due to their preference for propositional communication, elders may feel safer with a leader of whom they do not have to ask *many* questions. Millennials may feel safer with a leader of whom they can ask *any* question. Boomers and Gen Xers may expect leaders who are cutting edge and skilled because of their preference for a tinge of skepticism and intellect. Gen Z may be looking for the same thing in their leaders as they are in their communicators—a relational person.

Creating an intergenerational church starts with a leader who embraces intergenerational representation at every level, which could be accomplished through team leadership. The benefit of a team is that no one individual must possess all needed leadership attributes. Established leaders can embrace emerging leaders who are strong in areas they are not. Emerging leaders can trust established leaders and appreciate their experience and wisdom. As a result, the church, as the family of God, will be influenced by people from every age and stage of life.

Evangelizing Intergenerationally

The Christian mandate to share the gospel will remain intact until the Lord returns. It is a timeless mandate. Every generation of believers will be expected to evangelize their own along with the one that follows. What is reassuring is that the message of the gospel has already been outlined. It is static and cannot change. What is unnerving is trying to determine how best to communicate the ageless gospel in a moment in time or era in time.

In each chapter dedicated to the current living generations, I aimed to express the gospel in that generation's language. The gospel, as expressed in John 3:16, was presented uniquely to each of the generations. It is important to note that these snippets came from messages that were designed for evangelization through preaching. There is a difference in presenting the gospel to a group than to an individual. However, the same wisdom applies when evangelizing to one Gen Zer as it does when you evangelize to a group of them. Relational connection is the expectation despite the number of Gen Zers you are sharing with. The same is true for each generation and its communication preference.

Discipling Intergenerationally

The ABCs of salvation are incomplete without the D—discipleship. Acknowledging our sins, believing in Jesus' resurrection, and confessing him as Savior can only be reinforced by discipleship in the ways of Christ, especially with younger generations who are more dialogical and relational. These generations largely reject directive instruction for their lives. Religion, autocratic leadership, and propositional preaching all seem to be interrelated in younger minds. Jesus said, "I am the way, the truth and the life; follow me." Young Christians crave the way far more than they desire affiliation. Thus, a desire to be discipled in the ways of Christ will supersede any desire to be a member of a church. In Barna's study *The Connected Generation*, which examined the beliefs and values of young adults in twenty-five countries, young Christians consistently voiced a desire for their faith to permeate all aspects of their lives rather than be contained in church activities. About half strongly felt that, because of their beliefs, it was important that they "stand up against injustice," "give of their time and resources," and "have concern for the welfare of others." Theirs is not a culture that "plays" church. If they are going to take the counter-cultural step of being a Christian, they want to live out their faith wholeheartedly. They want to be formed in the *way* of Christ.

The generational language of a group will be critical as we seek to disciple people in that group because language employs words, concepts, and ideas that people use to get to know God. This will create tension between cliches and idiomatic expressions. Cliches, in general, trivialize God talk. Their nothingness misrepresents God's somethingness. Idioms, however, can be embraced and even added onto. To call Jesus the Rose of Sharon is to employ a biblical and true idiom. To call Jesus a friend of friends is to employ a biblical idiom relevant to social media culture. Neither of these expressions is cliché. Generationally polylingual discipleship sharpens the power of idioms while disregarding the tired cliches. To disciple intergenerationally is to be sharp on the idiomatic preferences of a generation.

Intergenerational discipleship requires learning the language, idioms, leadership preference, and culture of every generation and resourcing them through the life of your church. A simple way to do this is to have disciple makers from each generation lead groups within their own generation or the next down from them. A more sophisticated way to do this is to train every disciple maker to become generationally bilingual so that they are equipped to connect with another age group beyond their own. The most effective way to do this is to create a culture of generational polyglots who can train multiple generations in the ways of Christ.

I have mixed feelings about the efforts I made as a youth pastor to evangelize and disciple younger millennials and Gen Zers. I often focus more on the young people we did not thoroughly disciple even though parents typically express appreciation for how my team and I were able to connect their children to Jesus. In an effort to evangelize and disciple young millennials and Generation Z, we intentionally cannibalized our youth ministry's program to build relationships into the rhythm of our worship times.

We wearied ourselves spending thousands of dollars on youth conferences and trips, after which youth who appeared for the fun would disappear from the ministry's programming. And the ministry programming for high school and middle school was more like a teen version of what the adults did. Our Sundays featured large group gatherings and preaching. So, in an effort to better connect with students, we decided to keep the incoming class of sixth graders out of the main youth group and instead annexed them into a separate space on the church campus. The money we had been using for an elaborate conference was reallocated to resource them with discipleship curriculums. We also protected the ratios of leader to student by keeping it close to 1:8. This meant siphoning off some of the adult volunteers from the main group. Once we discontinued the conference, we put more focus on an annual lock-in and spring break trip and international mission trip. We essentially took the budget from our biggest event and used it to make our secondary and tertiary events better, after making a sacrificial investment into the redesigned programming. The redesigned programming focused on disciple making. A part of the high standard of disciple making was that our people (adult servant leaders and youth) could not miss more than 20 percent annually of the worship gatherings. This standard created a consistent environment where relationships could thrive.

After strategically cannibalizing the main group, its ratio was now closer to 1:25. My commitment was to be as present a youth pastor as I could be. At the time, our church had two youth pastors. Our sermons were very personable and relational. We wore our pastoral hearts on our sleeves. The few leaders who stayed with us in the large group threw their whole hearts at the current students while we threw our resources at the up-and-coming students. As the school years passed, our middle and high school large group became smaller by design. As seniors graduated, we did not bring in the next class of sixth graders. The initial group of sixth graders we had annexed stayed in the new discipleship model until eighth grade. We strategically separated the middle and high school and focused on discipling the younger ones.

Years after that experience I am reassured that it is possible to evangelize and disciple intergenerationally. We had boomer, Gen X, and millennial adults discipling millennial and Gen Z youths. The group I feared losing in the large group program we cannibalized and siphoned was not lost at all. The relationships formed there remain intact to this day. During the global pandemic, I was able to reconnect with Gen Z young adults who were in that large group, using Zoom to reunite biweekly for deeper Bible studies. Additionally, the strategic work of discipleship we did with the middle school students resulted in a deeper sense of kingdom success. Parents raved about how their tweens were growing. The feedback then and the fruit now are encouraging. You can do something like this, or even better, where you are currently serving.

Fellowshipping and Worshiping Intergenerationally

There are some churches who have removed children and youth from the adult worship and placed them in designed and dedicated spaces to improve their experience. In that sincere effort to improve the experience of the different generations, many a church has fallen into generational stratification by mistake. My goal is not to advocate for one approach over the other when it comes to where and when the different generations gather, but to reemphasize that fellowship and worship were intergenerational in Acts. Those biblical accounts of the early church affirm the power of intergenerational relationships in developing lasting faith.

In Acts 10, Peter was summoned to share the gospel with Gentiles. The Gentiles in Cornelius' house gathered to hear the gospel. In Acts 20, Paul preached in an upper room while the young Eutychus fell asleep and fell out of the window. It was after that young man was raised by Paul that those gathered continued their intergenerational worship and fellowship. The church from the first century to the twenty-first century has evolved from house churches to global church movements. It has evolved from micro churches to megachurches and back again. It has morphed from in-person gatherings to digital or hybrid gatherings that give its people options. The church has evolved from a small ragtag movement to an international organization. In all its evolution, there has also been some devolution. The church has devolved from an intergenerational fellowship to a splintered family unhappily sharing the same house until the younger ones are old enough to leave and never return.

The solution is in the church's origin. Whatever resources we expend to become intergenerational in our local churches will be worth its cost. Instead of the gray-headed church of elders bemoaning the loud music in that unorganized Gen Z church, efforts can be made to develop a reciprocal appreciation between both. I have felt the sting of serving young people in a congregation and watching them leave the church after graduating from the youth ministry. It should not be this way. We can do better. We must. Because worshiping and fellowshipping together validates a subgroup as an important part of the whole.

Intergenerational fellowship looks like people of all ages contributing their gifts and presence to key factors of the gathering. For some churches that might mean diversifying who leads worship in singing and playing instruments. For others it could mean giving space for teachers of all generations to teach the Word in some capacity. It could be youth serving youth. High schoolers discipling elementary students. It could look like middle school students coming into adult worship with their parents. Some older strategies in my church's tradition included junior deacons, youth choirs, youth ushers, and a youth ministry leadership advisory team. I served in all these spaces. When only one generation is affirmed in contributing its gifts, the other generations become spectators. We improve intergenerational fellowship when we refuse to relegate any group among us to spectate. We become intergenerational when every group is empowered to participate.

Ministering Intergenerationally

Ministry is another drumbeat in the rhythm of the twenty-first century church. Doing tangible good for others in the name of Jesus is the essence of ministry. An intergenerational church will be marked by people of all age groups functioning and influencing their major ministry endeavors. This can be done practically too. Perhaps a generational quota on international mission trips would help, or when subdividing the seats of influence in committees for special ministry events, such that each generation is at the table.

Before venturing to know what areas of ministry appeal to each generation, it would be helpful to host focus groups. A discussion group of a small representation of each generation will give church leaders critical insight. Church leaders will be able to hear from the generation and better understand how best to employ them in the work to be done. It is amazing how a little food and prayer can create an environment for focus groups to share. Over the years I have researched how to host focus groups and hosted many to assist my church in understanding our people. Here are some pointers I have learned to maximize the power of a focus group:

- Involve people by invitation only. This heightens their sense of appreciation in being involved in something important.

- Have release forms prepared. People should know, before participating, the extent to which their words and likenesses will be used.

- Be selective about the place. Pick somewhere quiet, well lit, and undisturbed by outside interruptions. The place can also be creatively picked to stimulate discussion.

- Have good food. It does not have to be gourmet, but it should be good and plenteous.

- Develop open-ended questions. Ask questions that stimulate discussion, not questions that force the group into a preconceived assumption.

- The facilitator should have only a handful of questions to ask. This keeps the facilitator engaged in following the discussion and its unpredictable nuances.

- Record the focus group. Having an audio or visual recording will make it easier for transcription software to capture words.

- Have a notetaker in the room. Get a skilled typist to capture sentiments. These notes can be compared to the transcription to refresh your memories.

- Scour the notes for salient themes and recurring thoughts. Identify and isolate these so that the good stuff from the group is relayed. Software can help with this.

- Create a compelling report of the insights from the group. This will help church leaders see how focus groups can inform strategy. This will communicate the narrative that the transcript captured in raw form.

■ Thank those who participated in a tangible way. Handwritten notes are powerful for this gesture.

To have an intergenerational value pervade a congregation's ministry, it is vital that every generation be seen in spaces where any generation is seen. Every generation must be recruited to serve in capacities that any generation is recruited to serve in. This endeavor may unearth the inherent ageism in many churches. It will also give each church a chance to crucify ageism so that a vibrant intergenerational congregation can grow in its place.

During the pandemic, our church increased its generosity and ministry to the community. I was tasked with partnering with other millennial leaders from our congregation to connect our church with community organizations. Our team scoured the city to find millennial-led organizations with a clear mission. We established partnerships through financial donations and providing people to help with that organization's endeavors. Our strategy was to recruit members of our church from every generation to participate in ministry in the community. We have built self-containing showers, harvested crops, made hot sauce, and hosted a back-to-school supply giveaway. We partner with organizations that serve the homeless, hungry children, families of children with disabilities, and ex-convicts reentering society. We partner with a charter school too. The strategy of having millennials in the church partner with millennial-led community organizations by leveraging the generosity and service of people from every generation is the essence of intergenerational ministry.

And this idea was not just a hunch. It was inspired by insight from a focus group hosted years ago.

Conclusion

If It's Too Hot in the Kitchen

The heat in the kitchen is turning up, isn't it? Every pastor and preacher can feel it. There is already inherent difficulty in cooking up delectable sermons on a regular basis. But, in a vacuum, preparing spiritual nourishment for people's souls is a manageable heat. It is the added pressure of the culture that makes people's satisfaction a moving target. Demographic complexities like gender, socioeconomic status, political leanings, ethnicity, and generational groupings make it hard to serve sermonic food that satisfies everybody.

The reflex of some preachers is to disregard those unsatisfied with their preaching as apostate. Paul's admonition to Timothy clearly stipulated the pattern of the apostate. They turn their ears from the gospel to false teachings. It is not apostasy, however, to slide back and get up from a spiritual table when the food is tasteless. And different people groups have unique taste buds. The pressure comes in learning how to prep and season our sermons differently so that they appeal to the different generations.

Recent events and the resulting response of each generation should indicate to us that the heat in the kitchen is rising. The increase of women in roles traditionally held by men, the murder of George Floyd, and the 2016 and 2020 presidential elections have impacted what people expect from their preachers.

Women in Key Roles

The twenty-first century has not brought about women's equality as speedily as it could have, but feminism has come a long way from its inception. Womanism, the fight for issues distinct to women of color, has also celebrated major strides forward. Increasingly, women are being seen in roles that more traditionally belonged to men. Vice President Kamala Harris is the first female and ethnic minority to occupy the VP's office. Jennifer Welter, Kathryn Smith, Katie Sowers, and Kelsey Martinez are climbing the coaching ranks in the NFL. Becky Hammon is the first woman to assume the role of a head coach in an NBA game. Women are refereeing professional men's sports and commentating on the games as they unfold. Shonda Rhimes, Courtney Kemp Agboh, and Lena Waithe are the geniuses behind some of TV's great shows.

Women have been running businesses of all sizes and will continue to do so. The rise of women to seats of power may be an adjustment for older generations, but it is the norm for younger ones. There is pressure then for us to include women and the issues that are unique to them in our preaching. Women deserve to be honored and well represented as joint heirs of Christ.

George Floyd

The eight minutes and forty-six seconds a White police officer kept his knee on the back of George Floyd's neck shook America and the world. In 1955, Mamie Till left the casket of her son open for all to see what had happened to him in the Mississippi Delta.

Photos in the newspaper exposed the world to Emmett's brutal murder after it happened. However, footage taken by camera phones let the world watch as breath and life left Mr. Floyd's body. The response to his murder turned up the heat in the kitchen. Millennials and Gen Zers took to the streets of Minneapolis. A multiethnic group gathered to protest, sparking similar protests across major cities in the United States. Any preacher seeking to nourish the souls of millennials and Gen Zers, especially in major cities, would be wise to understand their perspective on social justice. For preachers in the Black community, there may simply be a need to recall how their generation fought during the civil rights movement. For preachers in the White community, there may be more ground to cover as its younger generations could be more concerned about social justice than its older generations may have been.

The 2016 and 2020 Presidential Elections

The events surrounding the 2016 election revealed that many preachers cared more about politics than people. Many politicians within the Republican Party were more willing to speak honestly of the character of their candidate than pastors were. By the time of the 2020 election, many preachers had lost credibility while some dug their heels in deeper. The generations are watching and responding. The 2020 election results turned up the heat in the kitchen. Some are calling it the last stand for boomers. Others acknowledge the voting power wielded by younger generations. The pressure on preachers now is mounting. How do we honor the president if the person is dishonorable? How do we guide our congregation with the wisdom they will need to vote? How do we engage generations who see politics differently? My simple advice is to emphasize people over politics. But neither people nor politics are simple. Remember the goal is not always to agree but to understand. The victory is not in winning the political debate, but in winning the heart of a person or generational group.

Is It Too Hot? Well, Get O.U.T.

If it is too hot in the kitchen, get out. No, I am not suggesting you quit the preaching ministry. Although I can understand established leaders who see far enough around the corner to begin strategizing retirement. That is wisdom, but quitting is not. The o-u-t in "get out" is an acronym for you to meditate on as you seek to apply all that this book has stimulated in your heart. Get *Openness*, *Understanding*, and a *Team*. When these exist in our ministries, we get out of our flesh, we get out of silos, we get out of individual ministry heroics. We get our egos out of God's way and keep our inherent personal limits from limiting our preaching and our church.

Openness is required of the mind, heart, and arms. An open mind will listen, especially when it does not agree. An open heart will love, especially when it is afraid. And open arms will welcome, even when the person differs from you. Although many theological matters are closed, we should not be closed if we want the generations to remain open to the truth.

Understanding is offered before it should ever be expected. In a spirit of humility, understanding should never be demanded. It cannot be attained without listening. Wise preachers will listen to how perspectives have changed, which can be done formally through focus groups and informally through cultivating a culture where honest insight flows up. This is critical for our ability to connect well with any generation other than our own.

Teams win championships. A head chef has a team of chefs in their kitchen with them. The heat in the kitchen is not just there because of the griddles and ovens. It also comes from the pressure chefs feel trying to meet the growing, impatient, and everchanging demands of the dining hall. Expectations, not pots of boiling water, make it hot in the kitchen. There is pressure on preachers to serve up sermons sufficient to satisfy people's hunger for justice, understanding, wisdom, and meaning. We should not try to meet the demands of this pressure alone. You may be the head chef, but a pastry chef has a unique skill set that you may not. Outfitting our team with people who can bring their unique abilities to the kitchen will increase the probability that every generation at the table can be well fed.

It is getting hotter in the kitchen. Before quitting, get openness, understanding, and a team. If that seems too high a cost to ensure the generations are spiritually fed, then consider the cross of Jesus. We fix our eyes on him, the one who died for the generations. We fix our minds on him, the one who loves the generations. We fix our hearts on him, the one who seeks the generations. We anchor ourselves in Jesus. He will fill our souls and inspire our hearts as we respond to these times with his truth. We can do it. He will do it through us.

Acknowledgments

I could not have written this book without the unwavering support of my wife. Eboni has given more grace than anyone for me to continue serving faithfully in ministry. Her sacrifices can only truly be rewarded by God in eternity, but I will try my hardest to reward her until death parts us.

To my sons, Dylan, Daniel, and Dixon, thank you for allowing Daddy so much time to read and focus. To my parents, Rhonda Michelle Hall and Darrell Nealy, I desire to always make you proud. To my grandparents, siblings, family, and friends, thank you for always believing in me and supporting this undertaking.

I am immensely grateful to Elizabeth Baptist Church. It was there I met the Lord, met my wife, discovered my call, and began to fulfill my life's purpose. To Dr. Craig L. Oliver Sr., you have been to me as Paul was to Timothy; I honor you now and always. Also, to the board of directors, executive staff, staff, collaborative preaching team, members, and especially the Conyers campus—thank you!

Thank you to Dr. Robert Smith Jr., Dr. Mark Gignilliat, and Dr. Piotr Malysz for affirming the value of this research. This work would not possess the same depth of insight without the wisdom and expertise of subject matter experts. Pastor Ray Bentley of Maranatha Chapel in San Diego; Dr. Efrem Smith of Midtown Church in Sacramento; Dr. Joseph Warren Walker III, pastor of Mt. Zion Baptist Church of Nashville and the International Presiding Bishop of FGBCFI; Rev. Josh Peters of Mountain Mission School in Grundy, Virginia; and Rev. Bianca Robinson Howard of Zion Baptist Church in Marietta, Georgia—thank you all!

I also want to thank personal friends who aided me in finishing strong: Dr. Aaron Parker, Dr. Ken Dove, Ashley Hargrett, Dr. Stephanie Caine, Rev. Jason Caine, Rev. Terrence Albritton, Dr. Anyee Payne, Dr. Antonius Skipper, Dr. Myra Sabir, and Dr. Kelvin Cochran, thank you.

Finally, to Brooke Hempell and the team at Barna, I am amazed by our collaboration. You saw value in my fledgling ideas. You loved this research as much as I did. What started as mine became ours. Thank you for many years of intelligent and credible service to the kingdom of God. Onward and upward, we go in Jesus' name.

Appendix A
About the Research

In addition to drawing on existing data sources and Barna studies conducted about the worldviews and religious practices of each generation, for this book my friends at Barna and I designed and conducted a research study of the five adult generations to provide evidence of the preferences and perspectives of these audiences. Barna surveyed 513 regular churchgoers (pre-Covid-19) and 488 unchurched US adults, evenly spread across the generations, in December 2020 and January 2021. Participants were selected to be representative of US adults by gender, ethnicity, education, and the region in which they live. In addition to asking for opinions on church experiences and pastors, we designed and conducted a few experiments that enabled us to test my hypotheses about each generation's communication style preferences.

In the first experiment, survey participants listened to audio excerpts from sermons delivered by different well-known preachers. One clip was from a preacher that typically aims their message to their generation and whose style embodies the hypothesized language, and another was randomly selected from preachers who tend to use different styles and appeal to other generations. Survey participants selected their favorite message. The selection of preachers used were male only, so that we would not have to figure out how to account for any bias respondents may have had against feminine voices, especially respondents of older generations. As you read though, you will see the names of multiple female preachers who epitomize the ability to speak the languages of the generations.

In a second experiment, participants read several variations of sermon excerpts—the ones presented in each of the chapters of this book—and ranked them in order of preference. They then highlighted the words and phrases that stood out to them as appealing or relevant. Both experiments serve to inform and confirm the unique communication style preferences of each generation and the most effective means for preaching the gospel in their native tongue.

Appendix B
How to Apply this Research

This book reads like a sociological book in the front and a theological book toward the back. But it seems like your research is saying the opposite of what you believe the Bible says about intergenerational churches." My friend Haydn Shaw said this to me as he was working on the foreword for this book. I'm glad that he did. In *Generational IQ* he contends that a church cannot reach all the generations. Thus, he suggests that a church should choose which one(s) they will reach and which ones they will not. If possible, a church could assist another congregation in reaching a cohort that it does not. I could not disagree more. I appreciate the wisdom of his admonishment, but I am hopeful that a church can close these generational gaps through practical and loving actions. To help close the gaps in our churches, here are a few practical steps you can take to apply the research in this book:

- Go to www.speakingacrossgenerations.com and take the Generational Language Assessment. This tool will help you gain clarity on which generations your communication appeals to most and least.

■ For pastors (get a trusted team together to)

▶ Think critically through how effective your current church programming is in making disciples of each generation.

▶ Develop creative ideas of how to make the preaching menu more intergenerational. One way is to take one homiletic idea and state and restate it according to the generational languages. That is what I did with John 3:16. The sermon snippets at the end of each generational chapter are all points from one sermon. Another way is to plan for certain sermons or series to be targeted at one or two generations. The other untargeted generations could benefit from watching how you engage with different cohorts about biblical content. The church congregation could learn to embrace selflessness as different groups are prioritized.

▶ Consider hosting focus groups of the different generations in your church. See pages 132 and 133 for guidance.

▶ Intentionally plan for worship services where all generations are present together.

■ For preachers

▶ If you have a generational niche, hone that language into fluency.

▶ Think about what language your role models and preaching mentors use.

▶ Intentionally write sermons that are shaped in the generational language where you are weakest in fluency.

The research shared in this book is not intended towards pessimism. The goal is realism that fuels optimism. Scripture is rich with intergenerational connectedness among the people of God (see appendixes C, D, and E). As we embrace the insight in this data, lets apply it with hearts inflamed by God's love to reach each generation with the gospel.

Appendix C
The Intergenerational God

I n the beginning God" (Gen 1:1) revealed himself to humankind as one who creates (Gen 1:1), speaks (Gen 1:3), sees (Gen 1:4), makes (Gen 1:26), rests (Gen 2:2), blesses (Gen 2:3), curses (Gen 3:14), and redeems (Gen 3:15, 21). Without God volunteering to reveal himself, humanity could not have come to know these things about its Creator. From the beginning it was not God's desire that knowledge of him remain only with Adam and Eve. Scripture's first command was to "be fruitful and increase in number" (Gen 1:28). The first promise in Scripture was that the woman's "offspring" would "crush" the serpent's head (Gen 3:15), meaning a child born of the woman would defeat her enemy. Talk of Adam and Eve's children begins to show that God was intergenerational from the beginning of time. He wanted what was revealed about him to the first generation to be passed down throughout the generations.

Scripture continues the intergenerational theme with the first genealogy in Genesis 4. To be clear, the purpose of genealogies in Scripture is primarily to trace the redemptive thread to Jesus.

They read like a family tree. But genealogies also trace God's plan for salvation. In Genesis 4, Scripture begins to trace the lineage of Jesus. After the birth of Jesus, genealogies end. This supports that their primary purpose was to trace Jesus' family lineage. Though Jesus is the primary purpose of genealogies, their presence in Scripture accomplishes so much more. One cannot read genealogies without seeing how the generations were important to God.

If not for genealogies, Bible readers would never have known the connection of how God's movement in the lives of Judah, Rahab, Ruth, and David were to keep Jesus' lineage alive. There are also obscure biblical characters, like Jabez, who are only known because of genealogies. Even unknown characters whose names are lost in the list were known by an intergenerational God. The point is that what Jesus accomplished was kept possible by the generations before him. Though he would perfectly reveal himself in Jesus, God revealed himself in each of the generations from Adam to Abram, from Abraham to David, and from David to Jesus.

That God is intergenerational is implied in the creation story and genealogies of Genesis. However, God proved himself to be intergenerational in how he revealed himself to the three forefathers of Israel. God revealed himself to each of them individually and introduced himself (Ex 3:6) as the God of all of them collectively. God made a covenant with Abraham in Genesis 12:1-3 and then reaffirmed the covenant to Abraham's son named Isaac in Genesis 26:3-4. Then God reaffirmed it again to Isaac's son named Jacob in Genesis 28:14-15. God personally reintroduced himself to and restated his promises in each generation. These three men and their wives became the forebearers of the nation of Israel. Abraham, Isaac, and Jacob were Israel's patriarchs, and God was pleased to be known as their God. He was no more Abraham's God than he was Isaac's. He was just as much Jacob's God as he was Abraham's. When he called Abraham, he already had Isaac and Jacob in mind. No generation can claim a closer relationship with God than the next. God wants to reveal himself to each generation in a unique way.

After the patriarchs passed on, God continued to be intergenerational in the way he related to their children. Joseph was the famed son of Israel who became the prime minister of Egypt. He and his brothers were the fourth generation from Abraham. God revealed himself to them by preserving them from a deadly famine. After the days of Joseph, there arose a generation of Israelites who did not know God. It was difficult for them to know God because they had been made slaves in Egypt. All the stories they heard about their grandparents seemed like mere fables. They had no proof of God's presence in their generation. So, they cried out to a God they hoped, but could not prove, existed. In response to their cries (Ex 2:24), God proved he is real, that he hears, and that he speaks. By doing so, he revealed himself to a new generation. Pink believes that the patriarchs' God was the God of the generation enslaved in Egypt and is the same God today. He says,

> It is as the God of Abraham—the sovereign Elector; the God of Isaac—the almighty Quickener; the God of Jacob—the long-suffering One; who is about to bare His arm, display His power and deliver His people. And in the same threefold character does He act today. The God of Abraham is our God the One who sovereignly chose us in Christ before the foundation of the world. The God of Isaac is our God—the One who by His own miraculous power made us new creatures in Christ. The God of Jacob is our God—the One who bears with us in infinite patience, who never forsakes us,

and who has promised to perfect that which concerns us (Ps 138:8).[1]

God introduced himself in each generation of old and reintroduces himself to each generation today. His intergenerational heart is clearly seen in his intergenerational covenant with Israel.

An Intergenerational Covenant

A covenant is like a contract, except it is more. A contract is a document that binds two parties to an agreement. Its function is to protect each party from the character flaws of the other. A covenant, however, is based primarily on character. You can have bad character and be in a good contract. A good contract would legally force a person with bad character to do the right thing. But you cannot have bad character and uphold a good covenant. If you benefit from a good covenant even though you have bad character, you have received grace. Grace is a gift a person receives that they do not deserve. Grace is bad for business, so business people need contracts. Grace is great for life because people need God's love. The promises God made to Abraham, Isaac, and Jacob formed a covenant. Abraham and Isaac were liars and Jacob was a trickster. These are bad character flaws. The covenant they enjoyed with God, however, was based on God's character, which is flawless.

The Abrahamic covenant belongs to each of them equally. From the first promise made in Genesis 3:15 about the woman's offspring, comes the specific promises made through the Abrahamic covenant. This affirms that from the beginning God desired for the faith of one generation to be passed to the next. However, Genesis is full of examples of how flawed humans failed to pass down their faith to the next generation. Right after Genesis 3, the first generation (Adam) did not do well to transfer knowledge of God to the second generation (Cain). The Abrahamic covenant then was a necessary reset. Isaac's faith in God is a continuation of his father's and mother's faith. Jacob's faith in God is a continuation of his parents' and grandparents' faith. Intergenerational faith was made possible through an intergenerational covenant established by God with the patriarchs.

God includes the intergenerational importance of the covenant with Abram by promising to make him into a "great nation" (Gen 12:2). When God brought Abram outside to look at the stars (Gen 15:5), He promised that the covenant would be intergenerational. God plainly told Abram that "the fourth generation" (Gen 15:16) would return to occupy the Promised Land. Even though only Joshua and Caleb returned to the land, God did not allow the rebellion of the majority of the fourth generation to cancel his promise to Abram because the covenant was based on God's character, not on that of his people.

There is another factor that supports the covenant being intergenerational: each generation was to adopt the sign of circumcision. Circumcision was an intergenerational symbol. God says,

"I will establish my covenant as an everlasting covenant between me and you and your descendants after you for the generations to come, to be your God and the God of your descendants after you. The whole land of Canaan, where you now reside as a foreigner, I will give as an everlasting possession to you and your descendants after you; and I will be their God." Then God said to Abraham, "As for you, you must keep my covenant, you and your descendants after you for the generations to come. This is my covenant with you and your descendants after you, the covenant you are to keep: Every male among you shall be circumcised. You are to undergo circumcision, and it will be the sign of the covenant between me and you. For the generations to come every male among you who is eight days old must be circumcised, including those born in your household or bought with money from a foreigner—those who are not your offspring. Whether born in your household or bought with your money, they must be circumcised. My covenant in your flesh is to be an everlasting covenant. Any uncircumcised male, who has not been circumcised in the flesh, will be cut off from his people; he has broken my covenant." (Gen 17:7-14)

For each generation, the covenant of God with the parents was supposed to be intentionally passed down to the children.[2] God had each generation of Israelite children in mind before Abraham ever had Isaac. When the nation had only one generation, God established a covenant with all that would follow. The terms and symbol of the covenant were intergenerational by design.

Furthermore, each generation of Israelites was independently responsible for keeping the terms of the covenant. Though he died in Egypt, Joseph believed that God would keep his promise. Joseph asked that his bones be exhumed and taken to the Promised Land. This was his verbal confession of faith in God. Joseph and his brothers were responsible for keeping the covenant and passing it to their children.

However, from Joseph's generation to Joshua's, there was a disconnect in covenant keeping. The generation after Joseph's failed to make the connection. The generation that Moses led through the Red Sea died in the wilderness. While they were in the wilderness, they did not circumcise their children. They did not pass the symbol of their faith down. They may not have passed down much faith at all. Still, God kept his promise by allowing their children to enter the Promised Land. Once in Canaan, God fully expected that generation to keep the terms of the covenant. In Joshua 5:2-9 the next generation had to get circumcised because the covenant and its symbol were intergenerational in nature. Joshua and Caleb were the only two alive from the generation who died in the wilderness. Thus, Joshua bore the responsibility of connecting the younger generation to the covenant with God through circumcision. Howard says,

> Circumcision was an original sign of the covenant with Abraham (Gen 17:11), and it was to be done for every male in every generation . . . an entire generation had now crossed the Jordan who were not circumcised. This episode marks the beginning of Israel's true identification with the land of Canaan, and it contrasts the present generation of Israelites very starkly with the preceding generation.[3]

Despite what the previous generation had or had not done, every generation was accountable to God to keep the covenant. The independent accountability of each generation to God's covenant is not only seen in the time of Joshua but also centuries later in Josiah's restoration of worship (2 Kings 23:3, 21-23) after reading the Law. Both Joseph and Josiah understood their responsibility to the intergenerational covenant. They led their generations well even though the generation(s) before them were irresponsible with the covenant.

Appendix D
An Intergenerational People

The Israelites were culturally and socially intergenerational. Perhaps because both their God and their covenant were intergenerational, it was expected that the Israelites would interact in a like manner. The responsibility of older generations to the younger generations was expected. God expected an intentional transference of his commandments to the next generation during times of organic engagement (Deut 6:7). There was an assumption that the generations would organically interact. Dinner together around the table or a stroll afterward created time for informal instruction. Still, the teaching of God's commands was to be done with diligence. If the generations were not expected to socialize together, informal teaching could not occur. Separating generations from one another is called generational stratification, which would have eliminated organic moments for teaching God's commands.

In addition to his commandments, God expected the older generation to tell the younger of his acts. It was important that younger generations learned what God said and did. In Joshua 4:1-9 there is a story of twelve stones being taken from the basin of the Jordan River. These stones were gathered as the people walked across the river basin on dry ground, witnessing an act of God. The stones were to be placed as a monument to recall that act, as a conversation piece that fostered intergenerational dialogue. When time passed and younger generations came along, they would see those twelve stones and ask what they represented, prompting parents to tell them the story. That story would center around God's mighty acts. It was assumed that children would inquire just as it was expected that parents would respond—so that God might be glorified.

Furthermore, one of the most vivid pictures of Israel as an intergenerational people is recorded in Ezra 3:8-13. The remnant of Israel that came out of captivity intended to rebuild the temple of God, a project that would be an intergenerational undertaking. The adult Levites were given the task of overseeing the work (v. 8). Leaders with their brothers and their sons collaborated. Some were builders and others were singers (v. 10). The response after the foundation was laid was telling of the difference in generational perspectives. The older generation cried out of sadness. The younger generation shouted with gladness. The same restorative act of God was seen differently through generational lenses. The older ones wept aloud because they remembered the first temple. The younger ones celebrated because they had been born as prisoners of war in a foreign country. They were happy to be standing on the soil of their people. They were glad to finally be home.

Each viewpoint was neither better nor worse, but each generation had a different perspective of a shared history. Whether older or younger, each returning generation could sing with certainty that God "remembers his covenant forever, the word that he commanded, for a thousand generations, the covenant that he made with Abraham, his sworn promise to Isaac, which he confirmed to Jacob as a statute, to Israel as an everlasting covenant" (Ps 105:8-10 ESV). The psalmist had every right to sing these words. Why? Because the covenant belonged to his generation too. The promise made to Abraham in Genesis remained valid for every generation of Israelites, even those who returned from exile.

God created the world to be intergenerational. He used his relationship with Israel as an example of how that looks. His choosing of Israel teaches us something about God. Choosing Israel displays his desire for all people groups. He desires for all ethnicities and generations to know him. God desires for each generation to teach the next about him, but even if they do not, he has a way of revealing himself over and again. Let's choose to allow God to reach the next generation because of us. If we do not, he will reach them despite us. We can choose to be used by applying intergenerational principles.

The Intergenerational Church

The church was meant to be intergenerational from its beginning. This spiritual organism was organized as an interracial, intergender, international, and intergenerational body. Faith in Christ unifies people across racial, gender, geopolitical, socioeconomic, and generational lines. Generations of Christians were to meet and listen together to the same teaching. They were to even reemphasize the teaching of the apostles through their intergenerational relationships. That is why Paul explains to Titus how the generations should interact (Titus 2:1-8). However, the fellowship of believers is harmed by the way the American culture emphasizes generational stratification.

Cultural influences on how the church functions in ministry may counteract the Spirit's unifying work. Webster explains, "God's purpose is that we not divide along ethnic, cultural, racial, social, gender, and generational lines."[1] The intergenerational work of the Spirit in the church is a fulfillment of the prophecy in Joel 2:28. Since the Spirit was poured out at Pentecost without regard to one's life stage, he continues to work in and through persons in the church despite their life stage. As a matter of fact, the Spirit intentionally uses generational differences and life stage experiences to add to the fabric of the church. Paul told Titus that the old were expected to nurture the young. The presence of the old within the church was to benefit the young who were also present. Ackerman describes the old as sixty-somethings and the young as twenty-somethings.[2]

The intergenerational church in the New Testament reflects the intergenerational people of Israel in the Old Testament. In both communities, the older were to be examples to the young. They were to emphasize the gravity of godliness upon the young. The older men were to display what it meant to be the master of oneself and provide examples to young men who were prone to waywardness.

The church still needs the credibility healthy intergenerational relationships bring to the gospel. That is why the preacher should learn the language of the generations and preach effectively to them. Perhaps then more churches would become what they were always meant to be. Jesus never intended for His church to belong just to the old. He did not establish the church just for the young. The church was meant to set the standard for the world as a truly intergenerational organization.

Appendix E
An Intergenerational Gospel

God's message to one generation was always expected to be passed on to and heeded by the next generation, even if that message was bad news or was sent to people who did not worship him. For example, God gave a lesson in humility to Nebuchadnezzar, a Babylonian king who refused to acknowledge God (Dan 4:28-37). That lesson in humility was expected to be heeded by his son Belshazzar (Dan 5:18-22). The only way the son would know of the lesson is if his father taught him. Teaching was the father's responsibility. Listening was up to the son.

God obviously expected the same from people who did acknowledge Him. He said through the prophet Joel, "Tell your children about it, let your children tell their children, and their children another generation" (Joel 1:3 NKJV). God wanted a message of warning to be passed to the next generation. The gospel is good news, a message of hope. If God demands that bad news be passed down, he certainly wants good news to be passed down.

The gospel is good news to every person and all people groups. Remember, it is helpful to view each generation as a people group.

Elders, boomers, Gen Xers, millennials, and Gen Zers have distinct cultures and speak different languages. Scripture has much to share about the gospel's ability to permeate every people group.

The Day of Pentecost was marked by the coming of the Holy Spirit and the miracle of tongues. Acts 2:5-11 depicts various people groups hearing the Word in their own language, simultaneously. The audience that experienced the miracle of tongues was a mixed bag. Although Pentecost was an annual Jewish festival, it attracted non-Jews too.[1] The festival also intentionally included lower-class people in its feasts.[2] The crowd was ethnically and economically diverse, yet their cultural differences did not stop the gospel from reaching them effectively. Luke lists at least fourteen different nations present that day. Thus, the crowd was also linguistically diverse. They all spoke differently. The linguistic diversity sets the context for the miracle of tongues. Under normal circumstances, their differences would have created a language barrier. But these were not normal circumstances. These were supernatural circumstances. Each people group heard the good news communicated in their native tongue.

That the gospel can reach any people group is also seen in Peter addressing Cornelius' house in Acts 10. This account proves that race is no barrier that the gospel cannot cross.[3] When God proved this, did he not also prove that there should be no cultural barrier to the gospel? No gender barrier to the gospel? No economic barrier to the gospel? If a Jew should not see a Gentile as unclean, should a boomer view a millennial as unreachable?

Have you noticed that churches today are full of people whose language the churches speak fluently? Have you also noticed that churches are empty of people whose languages the churches refuse to learn? The language churches speak reach people based on their ethnicity, education, and socioeconomics. However, a person's generational language is just as vital. This is why churches are made up of a majority of one generation. That church speaks to its generation. Each church roster proves that the generational lens impacts a person's receptivity to gospel communication. They just may not be consciously aware of how they tend to reach the people that they do. There is nothing wrong with a church reaching primarily one generation, so long as they do it intentionally. The issue comes when a church claims to want to become intergenerational while remaining multigenerational. They only want the other generations there to watch as another generation leads, serves, grows, and finds community.

The beauty of the gospel is that it is good news in every language, regional dialect, and generational tongue. The miracle of Pentecost was that people heard in their distinct language and dialect. The message of Pentecost was the gospel. Despite what language it is translated into, the message remains the same. Regardless of which dialect it is communicated in, it remains. No matter the rhetorical devices it employs, the gospel cannot change. The rhetoric used in preaching must change, but the rudiments must not. How the gospel is communicated must change. What is communicated as the gospel cannot change. The gospel is the truth.

Paul's commitment to the gospel holds us all accountable. The apostle says, "For I am not ashamed of the gospel, for it is the power of God for salvation to everyone who believes, to the Jew first and also to the Greek" (Rom 1:16 ESV). The ultimate end of preaching is for God to be glorified as people are saved. The rhetoric used in communication must be a servant to that end. The preacher serves God, the gospel, and then the people, in that order.

The gospel is essentially good news about a person—the person.[4] Any news preached without the birth, death, burial, bodily resurrection, ascension, and return of Jesus is not the good news.

An Intergenerational Medium: Rhetoric in Paul's Preaching

The call to preach the word is a call to be a herald, he who stands in the public square and announces, "Hear ye, hear ye." A herald is faithful to his king by being faithful to his king's message. The risk in preaching the gospel is that faithfulness to God can be ridiculed by the godless as foolishness.[5] This risk is increased at a time when intellectual honesty is necessary. However, it is possible to be evangelistically faithful while also being intellectually honest. Not only is it possible, but it should also be practiced.

Paul gave an imperative to Timothy that applies to all preachers—preach the Word (2 Tim 4:2). Paul's imperative includes the content of the message. Ackerman says,

> The usual direct object of the verb preach is Christ, the Word, or the gospel (2 Cor 4:5). The Word (*logos*) is shorthand for the gospel, the 'good news' of Jesus Christ (2 Tim 2:9; 1 Tim 4:5; and 2 Tim 2:15) . . . Timothy should guard the deposit of the gospel (1 Tim 6:20; 2 Tim 1:14) and proclaim it accurately.[6]

The divinely chosen medium of communicating God's words to humanity is preaching. This cannot and will not change. Though a multitude of mediums should be employed in service of the gospel, none should replace preaching as the primary medium of gospel communication. The arts, technology, and books are all important gospel mediums. However, preaching is the primary gospel medium.

Rhetoric is the method a person uses to persuade another to change their beliefs. Reasoning is how one thinks about a subject. Paul's reasoning depicts his willingness to dialogue. Paul's rhetoric depicts his skill for intentional communication. Writing about Acts 17, Gartner says,

> Two different sides of Paul's missionary activity appear in this 17th verse. On the one hand he preached in the synagogue of the Jews, and spoke there according to the practice obtaining throughout the Acts; on the other, he spoke to the people he met with in the Agora. This second method was not peculiar to Paul; Socrates had used it long before him; and we can presume that a large number of propagandists and wandering preachers or philosophers roamed, in his own time, through the very tracts that he crossed on his missionary journeys. Paul therefore adopts this old form to enable him to convey his message. We can also venture to assume that, not only in Athens but everywhere on his journeys where it was necessary, he followed the preaching method characteristic of the Cynic-Stoic diatribe.[7]

Paul's rhetoric was on display in the context of his philosophically diverse audience.

In Acts 17 Paul addressed the Stoics and Epicureans. The Stoics lived in tune with nature, believing God to be the world-soul. They were pantheistic.[8] Paul's audience was also made up of Epicureans, who, named after Epicurus, ascribed to a life full of pleasure and peace. They aimed to live without pain and avoid superstitious fears.[9] Together these two erroneous philosophies sound like the conclusions of many post-Christian thinkers. Paul displayed what it means to be rhetorically omnilingual. That means he was able to be flexible in his persuasion. He did this by speaking the language of Jews and Gentiles. He could speak to both Stoics and Epicurean. If Paul could speak multiple cultural languages simultaneously, then you can connect with the boomer and the millennial simultaneously. The rhetorical flexibility of Paul did not dilute the gospel of its authority.

Paul was Socratic in his approach, meaning he was intentional in his communication. We must employ rhetorical devices that best communicate the gospel to contemporary ears and hearts. This means thinking about what cultural factors influence the minds of listeners. The generation a person was born in is one of those key factors.

According to Paul, it is definite that people will turn away from an effectively preached truth because their ears are itching. But it is also possible that people may turn away from an ineffectively preached truth because their ears are searching for something with more substance. How many people have turned away from a poorly preached gospel, thinking they wanted nothing to do with Jesus? How many have wrongly assumed that because the preacher was stale, Jesus must be boring? How many still think that, because the preacher could not connect with them, Jesus is not the answer for them? Even still, how many have heard a great gospel message but failed to approve of it because it was not contextualized into their generational tongue? Paul is a great example of how to contextualize the gospel. He adjusted how he explained the gospel without changing its content.

Paul's reasoning and rhetorical approach to the philosophers in Athens (Acts 17:16-34) give insight for the intergenerational communicator. Paul engaged the philosophers in thoughtful dialogue about the differences of their beliefs. He could not presume to engage in such mental exchange without a trained mind, which we know Paul possessed because he described himself as "a Pharisee" (Phil 3:5). He also recounted his years being reared by Gamaliel (Acts 22:3). Although he willingly jettisoned the social gain his credentials could earn him, he continued with a mind trained in the Law. After meeting Jesus on the road to Damascus, Paul's trained mind became conjoined with a heart set ablaze by passion for the gospel. The Christian preacher needs a trained mind and emblazed heart to engage people in dialogue about their varying philosophies. Gone is the day when uneducated congregations unwittingly accept at face value all that is shouted from a pulpit. This fact should not rattle the preacher but should move their preaching to engage in more thoughtful dialogue. *Thoughtful dialogue beats religious monologue.*

The message of the gospel crosses all ethnic, social, economic, and generational lines. The medium of preaching has been chosen by God to reach any people group, anywhere, any time with the message of Jesus. The biblical personalities, their experiences, and God's dealings with them are ripe for our learning.

Notes

1 Generational Science and Its Many Benefits

[1] My pastoral experience started as the campus pastor of a church campus with a megachurch multisite context. Prior to 2020, my campus would be regularly attended by 350–500 people per weekend. Across five campuses, our church was attended by 3,500–5,000.

[2] "Glossary of Barna's Theolographics & Demographics," Barna Group Organization, updated January 20, 2016, www.barna.com/glossary.

[3] Linda Searing, "The Big Number: Millennials to overtake boomers in 2019 as largest U.S. population group," *The Washington Post*, January 27, 2019, www.washingtonpost .com/national/health-science/the-big-number-millennials-to-overtake-boomers -in-2019-as-largest-us-population-group/2019/01/25/a566e636-1f4f-11e9 -8e21-59a09ff1e2a1_story.html.

[4] Leslie Williams, *When Anything Goes: Being Christian in a Post-Christian World* (Nashville: Abingdon Press, 2016), xiv.

[5] Ken Baker, "Beyond People Groups: Why the Term Communities May Be Preferable," *Evangelical Missions Quarterly* 53, no. 4 (Winter 2017): 8, https://s3.amazonaws .com/missio-emq/EMQ_Volume_53_Issue_4.pdf.

[6] C. S. Lewis, *God in the Dock: Essays on Theology and Ethics* (Grand Rapids, MI: Eerdmans, 1970), 94.

[7] Haydn Shaw, *Generational IQ: Christianity Isn't Dying, Millennials Aren't the Problem, and the Future is Bright* (Carol Stream, IL: Tyndale House Publishers, 2015) 249.

2 Becoming a Generational Polyglot

[1] Andy Crouch, *Culture Making: Recovering Our Creative Calling* (Downers Grove, IL: InterVarsity Press, 2008), 37.

[2] Douglas D. Webster, *Outposts of Hope: First Peter's Christ for Culture Strategy* (Eugene, OR: Cascade Books, 2015), 131.

[3] Matthew D. Kim, *Preaching with Cultural Intelligence: Understanding the People Who Hear Our Sermons* (Grand Rapids, MI: Baker Academic, 2017), 4.

[4] Kim, *Preaching with Cultural Intelligence*, 10-11.

[5] Jeffrey D. Arthurs, *Preaching with Variety: How to Re-create the Dynamics of Biblical Genres* (Grand Rapids, MI: Kregel Publications, 2007), 148.

[6]John Tucker, ed., *Text Messages: Preaching God's Word in a Smartphone World* (Eugene, OR: Wipf and Stock, 2017), 85.

[7]Zack Eswine, *Preaching to a Post-Everything World: Crafting Biblical Sermons that Connect with our Culture* (Grand Rapids, MI: Baker Books, 2008), 100.

[8]William Hull, *Strategic Preaching: The Role of the Pulpit in Pastoral Leadership* (St. Louis, MO: Chalice Press, 2006), 46.

[9]Hull, *Strategic Preaching*, 46.

[10]Tucker, *Text Messages*, 106.

[11]Tucker, *Text Messages*, xvi.

3 Language Is More

[1]L. Susan Bond, *Contemporary African American Preaching: Diversity in Theory and Style* (St. Louis, MO: Chalice Press, 2003), 19.

[2]John Tucker, ed., *Text Messages: Preaching God's Word in a Smartphone World* (Eugene, OR: Wipf and Stock, 2017), xxi.

[3]Tucker, *Text Messages*, 5.

[4]Howard Gardner, *Frames of Mind: The Theory of Multiple Intelligences* (New York: Basic Books, 1983).

[5]Mark Smith, "Howard Gardner and Multiple Intelligences" (The Encyclopedia of Informal Education, 2002, 2007), accessed on October 14, 2021, https://p9cdn4static .sharpschool.com/UserFiles/Servers/Server_97729/File/St.Thomas%20Aquinas %20Catholic%20Secondary%20School/Staff%20Links/Ms.Whelton/Gardners%20MI %20by%20Smith.pdf.

[6]Timothy Keller, *Preaching: Communicating Faith in an Age of Skepticism* (New York: Penguin Books, 2016), 178.

[7]James Earl Massey, *The Burdensome Joy of Preaching* (Nashville: Abingdon Press, 1998), 34.

[8]Keller, *Preaching*, 15.

[9]Bond, *Contemporary African American Preaching*, 89.

[10]Tucker, *Text Messages*, xvii-xix.

[11]Bond, *Contemporary African American Preaching*, 8.

[12]Daniel Overdorf, *Applying the Sermon: How to Balance Biblical Integrity and Cultural Relevance* (Grand Rapids, MI: Kregel Publications, 2009), 20.

[13]Overdorf, *Applying the Sermon*, 31.

[14]Michael Duduit, "Expository Preaching in a Narrative World: An Interview with Haddon Robinson," *Preaching Magazine,* accessed December 11, 2018, www .preaching.com/articles/expository-preaching-in-a-narrative-world-an-interview -with-haddon-robinson.

[15]Based on Barna Group's definition of *generational cohorts.*

[16]Susan Donaldson James, "Second Adulthood: Experts Say If It's Not Scary, You're Not Growing," ABC News, November 2, 2007, https://abcnews.go.com/Business/LifeStages /story?id=3274901&page=1.

4 Good News for Elders

[1]Barna, *Barna Describes Religious Changes Among Busters, Boomers, and Elders Since 1991*, July 26, 2011, www.barna.com/research/barna-describes-religious-changes -among-busters-boomers-and-elders-since-1991.

[2]Research conducted by Barna Group, December 18, 2020–January 20, 2021, n = 513 churchgoers.

5 Good News for Baby Boomers

[1]Research conducted by Barna Group, December 18, 2020–January 20, 2021, n = 513 churchgoers.

6 Good News for Generation X

[1]"Criminal Justice Fact Sheet," Resource Library, NAACP, accessed October 14, 2021, www.naacp.org/criminal-justice-fact-sheet.

[2]Research conducted by Barna Group, December 18, 2020–January 20, 2021, n = 513 churchgoers.

[3]Tacitus, *The Annals: Book 15* (109 A.C.E.), 15.44.

[4]H. W. and F. G. Fowler, *The Works of Lucian of Samosata*, vol. 4 (Oxford: Clarendon Press, 1949), quoted and cited by Gary R. Habermas, *The Historical Jesus: Ancient Evidence for the Life of Christ* (Joplin, MO: College Press, 1996)

[5]Josephus *Ant.* 18.3.3, accessed October 14, 2021, http://penelope.uchicago .edu/josephus/ant-18.html.

7 Good News for Millennials

[1]Research conducted by Barna Group, December 18, 2020–January 20, 2021, n = 513 churchgoers.

8 Good News for Generation Z

[1]Research conducted by Barna Group, December 18, 2020–January 20, 2021, n = 513 churchgoers.

9 The Family of God

[1]Douglas D. Webster, *Outposts of Hope: First Peter's Christ for Culture Strategy* (Eugene, OR: Cascade Books, 2015), 153.

10 Intergenerational in Everything We Do

[1]Kevin and Jackie Freiberg, "20 Reasons Why Herb Kelleher Was One of the Most Beloved Leaders of Our Time," *Forbes* magazine, January 4, 2019, www.forbes.com/sites /kevinandjackiefreiberg/2019/01/04/20-reasons-why-herb-kelleher-was-one-of -the-most-beloved-leaders-of-our-time/?sh=5ed0a13db311.

[2]Jimmy Long, *The Leadership Jump: Building Partnerships Between Existing and Emerging Christian Leaders*, (Downers Grove, IL: InterVarsity Press, 2009), 16.

[3]Long, *The Leadership Jump*, 15.

Appendix C: The Intergenerational God

[1]Arthur W. Pink, *Gleanings in Exodus* (Chicago: Moody Press, 1962), 25.

[2]James Murphy, *A Critical and Exegetical Commentary on the Book of Genesis* (Boston: Estes and Lauriat, 1873), 310. Murphy says, "It is worthy of remark that in circumcision, after Abraham himself, the parent is the voluntary imponent, and the child merely the passive recipient of the sign of the covenant. Hereby is taught the lesson of parental responsibility and parental hope. This is the first formal step in a godly education, in which the parent acknowledges his obligation to pursue all the rest. It is also, on the command of God, the formal admission of the believing parents' offspring into the privileges of the covenant, and therefore cheers the heart of the parent in entering upon the parental task. This admission cannot be reversed but by the deliberate rebellion of the child."

[3]David M. Howard Jr., *Joshua, The New American Commentary: An Exegetical and Theological Exposition of Holy Scripture*, ed. E. Ray Clendenen, vol. 5 (Nashville: Broadman & Holman Publishers, 1998), 147.

Appendix D: An Intergenerational People

[1]Douglas D. Webster, *Living in Tension: A Theology of Ministry* (Eugene, OR: Cascade Books, 2012), 2:106.

[2]David A. Ackerman, *1 & 2 Timothy, Titus: A Commentary in the Wesleyan Tradition*, New Beacon Bible Commentary (Kansas City, MO: Beacon Hill Press, 2016), 422.

Appendix E: An Intergenerational Gospel

[1]Gerald L. Stevens, *Acts: A New Vision of the People of God* (Eugene OR: Pickwick Publications, 2016), 42.

[2]Stevens, *Acts*, 55.

[3]Ernst Haenchen, *Acts of the Apostles: A Commentary* (Philadelphia: Westminster Press, 1971), 351.

[4]Douglas J. Moo, *The Epistle to the Romans* (Grand Rapids, MI: Eerdmans, 1996), 67.

[5]John Stott, *Romans: God's Good News for the World* (Downers Grove, IL: InterVarsity Press, 1994), 60.

[6]David A. Ackerman, *1 & 2 Timothy, Titus: A Commentary in the Wesleyan Tradition*, New Beacon Bible Commentary (Kansas City, MO: Beacon Hill Press, 2016), 364.

[7]Bertil Gartner, *The Areopagus Speech and Natural Revelation* (Uppsala, Sweden: C. W. K. Gleerup, 1955), 46.

[8]F. F. Bruce, *The Book of Acts* (Grand Rapids, MI: Eerdmans, 1988), 330.

[9]E. M. Blaiklock, *The Acts of the Apostles* (Grand Rapids, MI: Eerdmans, 1959), 138.

About the Author

Darrell Hall was born and raised in Atlanta, Georgia. He received Christ as his Savior and Lord at a young age and was baptized at the Elizabeth Baptist Church (EBC). In September of 2003, at age seventeen, Darrell accepted his calling into the ministry. Ordained January 24, 2015, Darrell currently serves as the campus pastor of EBC's campus in Conyers, Georgia. Darrell received a bachelor of arts in religion in 2008, a master of arts in Christian studies in 2010, and a master of divinity in 2016 from Luther Rice Seminary. He finished a doctor of ministry degree from Beeson Divinity School at Samford University in December 2019.

Darrell Hall is a man of faith who looks humbly and expectantly at what his future will bring. Through online public speaking courses, writing, pastoring, preaching, and speaking, he is investing in others. The joy of his life is his best friend and the wife of his youth, Eboni. They are the parents of sons Dylan Elijah, Daniel Elisha, and Dixon Emmanuel.

Instagram: @iamdarrellhall
Twitter: @iamdarrellhall
Website: www.iamdarrellhall.com
YouTube: www.youtube.com/c/DarrellHallSpeaks